Classic Customs and Lead Sleds

Bo Bertilsson
Foreword by Ken Gross

MBI Publishing Company

First published in 2001 by MBI Publishing Company, 729 Prospect Avenue, PO Box 1, Osceola, WI 54020-0001 USA

MBI Publishing Company books are also available at discounts in bulk quantity for industrial or sales-promotional use. For details write to Special Sales Manager at Motorbooks International Wholesalers & Distributors, 729 Prospect Avenue, PO Box 1, Osceola, WI 54020-0001 USA.

Library of Congress Cataloging-in-Publication Data
Bertilsson, Bo.
    Classic customs and lead sleds / Bo Bertilsson.
      p. cm.
    Includes index.
    ISBN 0-7603-0851-9 (pbk.)
    1. Hot rods. 2. Automobiles—Customizing—California. 3. Automobiles—Decoration. I. Title.

TL236.3.B46   2001
629.228'6—dc21   00-135003

Edited by John Adams-Graf
Designed by Arthur Durkee

On the front cover: Rick Dore used a lot of late 1960s and early 1970s Caddy parts to update the car he evenually would name Majestic. Looking like a king's Caddy when it first rolled in at the Oakland show in 1996, it went on to win numerous awards during the season.

On the frontispiece: Marcos Garcia's Hundreds of floating, chromed drawer knobs deck the grill of Marcos Garcia's 1963 Buick Riviera. Garcia, who has painted award-winning customs for many of the hobby's biggest names, built his own show-winning Buick over a period of years as an after-hours project at the Lucky 7 shop in Antioch, California.

On the title page: Mike Young's abalone pearl-painted '60 Chevy was built by Gary Howard and designed by the famous rock and blues guitar player Jimmie Vaughan (that's Vaughan's '51 Chevy in the background). Howard started by chopping the top 3 inches before he cleaned all emblems and handles from the body. In true customizing fashion, he modified the front end by adding headlights from a 1963 Olds, a bumper off a 1959 Chevy, and a custom grille. The whole package earned its place among famous customs when it received the Barris d'Elegance Award at Oakland Roadster Show. *Steve Coonan*

On the back cover: Top: This rare 1957 shot shows a neat group of six Watson-painted customs. The most famous car in the lot is Jack James' 1957 Buick (foreground). Watson gave this car a full flame treatment. The famous painter is sitting right in the middle of this pack of young custom-owners. *Jim Potter* **Lower right:** Rick Dore thought that a LaSalle grille was too commonplace among customizers so he decided that a '40 Packard grille would be the perfect way to set his '36 Ford apart from the rest. As the crowning touch, Rick adorned the front end with a pair of 37 Buick headlights welded to the fenders.

Printed in China

Table of Contents

Ken Gross, who has roots in customs and hot rods, is the director of the Petersen Museum in Los Angeles, California. His own time-perfect '32 roadster won the *Bruce Meyer Award* for best nostalgia hot rod at the Grand National Roadster Show in San Francisco in 1999.

Foreword

OK, I'll admit it, although most of the cool cars I've owned have been hot rods, and they've all been Fords, my first car was a '50 Chevy convertible—and it was a custom. It's unbelievable now, but I had saved up and my parents let me buy it in 1956 (for $150!) when I was 15. I couldn't legally drive for another year, so I kept it at my grandmother's. In those days, I read *Hot Rod* and *Car Craft* and on the East Coast we had *Rodding and Restyling*. As kids, we were sure that we could design cars better than anyone else in Detroit could. Within weeks, my stovebolt was nosed and decked, the door handles were filled, and then I got really ambitious and molded in the rear fenders.

Everything I thought I knew came from car magazines and ogling the other guys' cars at school. Soon, the stock taillights were scrapped, the holes were filled, and '52 Buick lights were mounted horizontally in the panel below the deck lid. Slim's Auto Body in Lynn, Massachusetts, re-did some of my shoddy early work with lead when the fiberglass cracked. Later, I frenched the headlights with '52 Ford rims. Lowering blocks in the rear and cut coils in front brought it down to a cool level. So what if it rode like a tractor? John "Shag" Sharrigan of Allston, Massachusetts' famed Nomads Club, fabricated a split exhaust system and a homemade dual manifold for the car. My father did the upholstery and a rear seat tonneau cover in black-and-white Naugahyde. I didn't think it was much of a ride in comparison with a few of the guys' chopped Mercs, but it was pretty sanitary, and even in primer it was better than driving your father's Plymouth.

Custom cars were pretty common in the Boston area when I was in high school. I was a member of the Salem, Massachusetts, Choppers and I still own my old club plaque. Because Massachusetts' rotten winters discouraged open-wheeled roadsters and coupes, only a few brave guys built them. Mostly, we had primered shoe-box Fords and we fantasized about California. One guy I knew even stole a pair of yellow "Cal plates" during a family trip in Los Angeles so that he could use them on his custom at car shows.

California was where it was really happening. I was sure every car on the streets of L.A.—or in exotic places with names like Tarzana and Pismo Beach—was a rod or a custom (you'd think that too if you read the "little books"). But we tried: my pal Lennie Legere built a radically chopped and lowered '49 Ford ragtop with canted Lincoln headlights, Edsel taillights, and split '55 Pontiac bumpers that made it into some of the magazines, along with Eddie Vargabedian's Olds-powered Stude coupe. Talk about hitting the big time!

Looking back, we had just as much fun using the crude welding skills we learned in high school shop classes, with smelly fiberglass cloth and resin bought from J. C. Whitney and with mail-order speed equipment from Lewie Shell, Ed Almquist, and Honest Charley, as the California kids who had cars built by the legends. We knew all the legendary names: do-it-yourselfers like Duane Stack were heroes, but the guys we really looked up to were Gene Winfield, Dean Jefferies, Larry Watson, Neil Emory, Clay Jensen, Joe Bailon, and the king, George Barris.

Today, John D'Agostino, Richard Zocchi, Rick Dore, and Jimmie Vaughan are keeping those great old custom traditions alive. They're way past the obligatory '49–'51 Mercs. They're applying lessons learned over decades to different cars from the same, and slightly larger, eras. Their rides still turn heads and the crackle of their exhausts make gray-haired guys smile and remember the hot August nights of a simpler era.

Bo Bertilsson has brought it all back in this book. Read it, dig the pictures, and see if it doesn't make you want to pick up a torch and take 3 inches out of that too-tall roofline. This book will take you back, and maybe you'll want to stay there. By the way, if you are wondering what happened to my old Chevy, I swapped it with a kid named Tom de Focce for his primered '40 Ford coupe, got involved with flatheads, and never looked back.

—*Ken Gross*
Manhattan Beach, California

One of the author's first cars was a '58 Edsel with a few minor modifications such as shaved handles, sunken antennas, and so on. This picture was taken in March 1967.

Preface

It all started for me in 1958, when I saw Bo "Gamen" Sandberg working on a '55 Mercury convertible that he had modified with opened-up rear wheel wells, a rolled pan in the rear, and a tube grille in the front. I thought it was amazing to see him sink two antennas in the front fender. When I later saw the car painted with a Larry Watson–style paneling job in turquoise, white, and gold, I was very impressed. At that time I had never heard of Larry Watson. I had gotten hold of some hot rod magazines before this had happened, but became interested in customs too.

A few years later, when *Rod & Custom* magazine was published in the larger format, I found one store in my hometown of Stockholm, Sweden, that imported U.S. automotive magazines. Each month, they carried 10 copies of *Rod & Custom*, so you had to be there as soon as they arrived, or you would not have a chance to buy one. It took a few months before I found out that they took orders and put them in an envelope with your name on it. No wonder I occasionally went home empty-handed when the store was all out. There were not many pages in that magazine, and my English was not as good as it should have been to read it, but the pictures and the captions were something that I pored over for weeks. More magazines followed, and I liked to check out the "how to" sections that George Barris and others contributed at the time. The first time I found a "how to" story on chopping the top (in this case a '55 two-door Chevy) I was stunned.

The first-ever hot rod show in Stockholm was held in the early 1960s, and it was in the part of town that I was living in with my parents. There were more customs than hot rods at the show, which took place over a weekend in a VW dealership showroom. My friends and I were there, checking out the dozen-or-so cars that were entered in the show. On Friday night, a couple of guys from the south side of town turned up with a mild custom '57 DeSoto, which we thought was about the wildest thing we had ever seen. The front end had the bumper removed and replaced by a hand-shaped tube grille, and all the chrome trim was cleaned off the body, including the door handles. These two guys didn't want to show us kids how they opened the doors. They played with us, and while we were looking at the guy standing by the door, who was pretending to do something, the other one was pulling the wire handle in the grille, which opened the doors. The 1960s were good times for both hot rod and custom building in Sweden, so more and more cars turned up at the big Stockholm show each winter.

I also remember the first time I saw a metalflake paint job (on a '49 Ford custom owned by a guy in Stockholm). It must have been in 1963 or 1964 when I first saw this Chevy-powered '49 Ford right outside where we lived. The V-8 sound and the glittering paint stopped me right in my tracks. It was really something special with that blue metalflake paint. In 1964, the first real hot rod show was arranged in Stockholm, and Bo Sandberg was involved with that as well as building some rods and customs. The show brought all of us that were into rods and customs together and gave us inspiration to build something.

I was still in school and didn't have any money to build a car, but I was reading all the magazines that I could get a hold of. In 1969, I was working and able to save some bucks to make my first trip to California and the Oakland Roadster Show. After seeing the real rods and customs at the show, I was very much pumped up and wanted to see more. I used the rest of my two-week trip to go to Los Angeles and visit all the shops I had read about, like George Barris' place in Hollywood, but I had no clue what I was getting into when I went to see Ed "Big Daddy" Roth. At his shop in Maywood there was plenty of stuff to see, and I met some people that day whom I still see now and then, including Roth himself. His message to me that day in February 1969 was, "Go home and get yourself a good camera and do some stories for my *Choppers* magazine." Said and done, and I started to get into photography.

By the time my first features landed on Roth's desk in Maywood, he had already sold the magazine.

I was not a happy camper the day the pictures were returned in the mail, but I didn't give up. I checked out the magazines on the market and found the first issues of Tom McMullen's *Street Chopper*, so I sent the stories to them instead. They ran my stuff right away, and I'll never forget the day when I saw my first story published. A few years later I started to do some stories for Bo Sandberg's then-new magazine, Colorod, and in 1973 I became the bike editor for the book. I also continued to do freelance material for the U.S. magazines, even when I later became the editor and owner of Colorod magazine. My good relations with McMullen Publishing led me to do more and more rods and customs for their magazines through the years. I met Tom Vogele during the time he was working for Boyd Coddington in the early '80s, and later he became the editor for *Street Rodder* magazine. It was also Tom and Jerry Weesner who created the idea of starting a sister magazine to *Street Rodder*, but about customs, and calling it *Custom Rodder*. I have done a lot of stories for them through the years, but since 1987 I have been based in California as a correspondent for the Scandinavian automotive magazines and am doing most of my work for the European magazines. I am very happy to be able to be right in the middle of the rod and custom center of the world, and work with my hobby full time. I still go back to my old hometown of Stockholm every summer to cover the best of the events for the U.S. magazines and write features on the top cars. Today, building customs is a growing business again, having nearly died out during the 1970s and early 1980s. It is getting much bigger now than it ever was in the early days. I would like to send a special thanks to MBI Publishing Co. for letting me do this book. It has been a pleasure to relive the moments when I took the pictures, and to meet all the great people involved in this hobby.

Acknowledgments

I would like to thank some people who made it possible for me to do this book. First of all, Thom Taylor, for giving me a chance to use some of the Larry Watson pictures from the Jim Potter collection. A thanks to Ken Gross for writing the foreword, and Gene Winfield, John D'Agostino, Richard Zocchi, and Steve Coonan for letting me use some of their pictures. I also wish to thank Cory Moore and Jimmie Vaughan for all their help. A special thanks to my son, Tim, Stig Sjöberg, and my mentor, the late Bo Sandberg.

—Bo Bertilsson

The 1957 Buick is the model that many custom builders prefer because it is simply a perfect starting point. A nose and deck job, followed by cleaning off the emblems and handles lends itself to lowering and whitewalls. The effect can be stunning—just like Walter Gibson's neat custom tuck and roll interior. This car is a great drive into the world of customs and lead sleds.

Gene Winfield

He is one of the living legends of custom car building, and is still building many trophy-winning cars for his customers. Gene Winfield got started in 1944 when he opened a shop in his hometown of Modesto, California, with two of his brothers. He had just returned from World War II and a tour of duty in the Navy. The three brothers mostly did regular bodywork and painting in their shop, but now and then they did some custom work as well.

In 1947 Gene opened his own Windy´s Custom Shop, where he did all kinds of modifications, bodywork, and painting. By 1955 it had grown to a much bigger shop, where he was doing prototype work for both Ford and Chrysler. The shop was also renamed with his full last name, "Winfield's Custom Shop."

Between the concept cars for the Detroit people, he was building custom cars for his regular customers. One that got plenty of publicity was *Rod & Custom* magazine's *Dream Truck*. Based on a '50 Chevy pickup, it was designed following the suggestions of readers. It was sectioned and chopped, and had a lot of modifications done to

The latest creation to come out of the Winfield Shop in Canoga Park is this wild '61 Caddy that he named "Maybellene" after the famous Chuck Berry tune. He put a lot of hours into replacing the top with a "Flat-top" from a '59–'60 GM four-door hardtop model. The top is also "buried" in the bodywork to get a chopped look. Both the windshield and the rear glass were dropped down in the sheet metal. *Gene Winfield*

It is hard to believe that Gene Winfield was already building rods and customs in 1944, right after he came home from the war in Europe. His favorite cars are the 1950s and 1960s big customs with fins, like the '61 Caddy "Maybellene" that he built, but many of the cars that he builds are still '49–'51 Fords and Mercurys. *Gene Winfield*

both the front end and the pickup bed. The front fenders were made from pieces of four Buick fenders, along with pieces from a stock Chevy. Late in 1954, one of the first Chevy V-8s that came out of the factory was dropped into the truck. The vehicle was painted pearl white, with candy purple scallops. It was wrecked some years later on the way to a show, but after being stored for many years, it came into the possession of Bruce Glasscook of Costa Mesa, California, who rebuilt it completely.

The first custom to gain Winfield national recognition was the *Jade Idol*, built in 1960 and based on a '56 Mercury. It took nearly two years to build and it was wild. Instead of chopping the car, he sectioned it and lowered the suspension all around. It was very hard to see what kind of car he started with because of the sectioning, which means that he took 4 inches out of the middle of the body. The front end was modified with dual frenched headlights, and the rear fenders were taken from a Chrysler. One of the most

To get a more modern take on the "Maybellene" project, Winfield and his staff used a Northstar four-valve Cadillac motor bolted to a modified S-10 700-R4 transmission. The engine looks like a big Hemi, but it is the late-model Caddy. Northstar specialist Alan Johnson modified the motor with Seville camshafts and the special manifold for an 890-CFM throttle body injection.

The steering wheel was made from clear and gold transparent Lucite that was laminated together and machined by Dekker Plastics of Chatsworth, California. With all the parts machined and hand-sanded, the steering wheel looks like a "glass wheel." Winfield likes to work with different materials and the steering wheel is a good example of that.

Winfield has built a few trucks for his own shop through the years, and this 1934 Ford truck was built in the early 1960s. It received an updated suspension, modern V-8 engine combination, and plenty of body modifications (including being chopped and channeled) before it was given a candy paint job. *Gene Winfield*

spectacular things with the *Jade Idol* was the blended candy paint job in pearl white over a deep candy green. Gene Winfield came up with that technique in 1957 when he was trying to blend two candy colors together. Winfield created a trademark with his faded, blended candy paint jobs, for which he is still well known today. When you see one of those faded candy paint jobs, you know who did it. Looking at those paint jobs, you will soon understand how hard it is to get the transparent candy in straight, even, blended lines. All the other big names in the custom building business have come to him for special paint jobs over the years.

The *Idol* won top awards at shows throughout the United States for years. In 1962 it won "Best Body Shop entry" at the NHRA Nationals at Indy. Another wild creation that Winfield built in the early 1960s was *Solar Scene*, a chopped '50 Mercury with a '53 Mercury windshield. The body was modified with sculpted wheelwells with stainless inserts, dual frenched headlights, and a handmade grille. Winfield painted the *Solar Scene* in a candy bronze with faded edges around the

The *Rod & Custom Dream Truck* was a nearly new '50 Chevy truck that was chopped and channeled. Big body modifications were done to both the front sheet metal and the pickup bed before it was painted in white pearl and purple candy. They also dropped a brand-new Chevy V-8 in the truck in late 1954, right after the factory released the engines for the '55 Chevys. *Gene Winfield*

One of the wilder '50 Mercurys that Winfield built during the early 1960s was this chopped version that he named *Solar Scene*. Most of the sheet metal on this car was modified, and the extreme-shaped wheelwells have stainless-steel inserts. Under the hood he used a Buick Nailhead engine and plenty of chrome. The Mercury was painted in a special mix of bronze candy shaded around the wheelwells. *Gene Winfield*

wheelwells. A new custom trick in the Mercury was custom-built seats that swung out with the power-operated doors.

After the Merc he built a couple of wild aluminum-bodied cars called *Strip Bar* and the most well known, *Reactor*, which was also a part of the *Bewitched* television series. He bought the *Reactor* back a few years ago and restored it in time for the 50th Oakland Roadster Show in 1999.

In 1962, Winfield was hired on a consultant basis by the model kit company AMT as a style designer. AMT was headquartered in Phoenix, Arizona, and in 1966 they hired him full time to run their new Speed and Custom Division shop. There they built all the full-scale cars for AMT´s 3-in-1 model kits, which would be the promotional vehicles for the models later. Through the work at the shop, he came in contact with both the film and television industries and built vehicles for series like *Man from U.N.C.L.E.* and *Star Trek*. Winfield also built a car for the *Dean Martin Show*, that was rolled on stage as a Camaro convertible, but was changed piece by piece into a '31 Chevy Roadster by dancers while Frank Sinatra sang.

In 1970, Winfield decided to open his own shop again, this time in North Hollywood, to be

The first custom that Winfield received national recognition for was this –'56 Merc named *Jade Idol* and built for LeRoy Kimmer. The body was sectioned 4 inches and the suspension lowered. Winfield frenched dual headlights in the front fenders and made a totally different grille. The *Jade Idol* had the first blended candy paint job that was ever done on a show custom. Since those days, it has become a trademark for Winfield. *Gene Winfield*

Dennis Renero came to Winfield's shop with a nearly brand-new '56 Olds, to have it customized. The unusual thing was that it was a four-door hardtop, and it was modified with dual Lucas headlights and a handmade grille. All door handles and emblems were cleaned off the body. Winfield painted it in candy. *Gene Winfield*

close to the movie and TV industries. In 1972 he built four "bubble cars" for the Woody Allen film *Sleeper*, and later he built many different cars for other movies.

Over the years, Winfield's cars have been featured in more than 20 movies, including *Robocop*, *Bladerunner*, and *The Last Starfighter*. Additionally, he built cars for television shows such as Batman and *Mission Impossible*. He has also done some very special vehicles for TV commercials, including one car for Chevrolet that was cut in half, front to rear, with both parts still drivable. He built another car from parts of 30 different cars for an insurance company that wanted to show that they could insure "any car." Another car was frozen in a big ice block, to be started a week later when the ice was chipped away.

For the last 20 years Winfield has also created many new parts for building customs, such as a '50 Mercury fiberglass front end with frenched headlights and other features. Another popular item is his fiberglass Carson top, which saves the builder many long hours and makes it easier to cut the roof off of a sedan to make a convertible.

At an age when most people would wind down to take it easy, Winfield is still building cars for his customers and spraying his fabulous faded candy paint jobs on some of the most spectacular customs of the day. He also builds cars for himself: the latest is a '61 two-door Cadillac hard-top that he named "Maybellene" after the girl in the famous Chuck Berry song. The Caddy was modified with a flat '59–'60 GM four-door hard-top roof, lowered by sinking the windshield and the rear glass into the body instead of chopping it. This way he didn't have to make a new, very expensive windshield for the car. The doors were modified with special flush-mounted power flip-up mirrors, and also remote door openers. He extended the rear fins 5 inches and also extended the lower fins together with the '62 bumper that was used. The hood, which was extended over the windshield wipers, is now operated with two electric screw jacks. Two big Optima batteries were installed as well.

Lenny Eriksen had a '56 Chevy built by Winfield in the late 1950s. The two-door sedan received a radical chop before the body was cleaned of door handles and emblems. The front end was modified with a '57 Chevy bumper and a '53 Chevy grille. *Gene Winfield*

In 1956 Winfield built this '50 Ford Convertible for Jon Van DerKamp. It was given a mild modification with a new look to the front end with the frenched headlights and a Cadillac grille. Smooth bumpers and scallop paint are typical for the 1950s. *Gene Winfield*

LeRoy Gowart had his '50 Ford customized by Winfield a couple of times during the mid-1950s. The picture shows the car after the last modifications in 1957. The front fenders and grille were modified with dual Lincoln headlights and handmade pieces. Wheelwells were cut out, and the caps came from a '57 Plymouth. *Gene Winfield*

To make it possible to use a '62 Cadillac deck lid, he reskinned the '61 deck lid with the '62 sheet metal and then extended the lip with a custom-made panel, to go all the way down to the bumper. The headlights are NOS British Lucas "Flamethrowers." To get a different interior look, Winfield grafted in a '60 Olds dash and made a special "glass" steering wheel from machined plastic pieces. The upholstery was finished in beige leather. When it came to the engine, he wanted something more modern under the hood, so he chased down a Caddy Northstar V-8. With the engine modified by Northstar expert Alan Johnson, it now has Seville STS camshafts and an 890-cfm injection throttle body made by Accufab. Before the engine was dropped in the car, it was bolted to a modified Chevrolet S-10 700R transmission. Jim King fabricated a set of stainless-steel headers, together with a 2-1/2" exhaust system exiting through Flowmaster mufflers. To get a nice ride in the car and still get it super-low, Winfield and his guys installed an Air Ride Techniques air suspension. As always, the new car was finished with one of Winfield's trademark blended candy paint jobs, this time in yellow and gold.

Gene Winfield is definitely one of the fathers of customizing, having participated in the California rod and custom car culture since the 1940s. Through the 1960s he was part of two projects that won the America's Most Beautiful Roadster award: Tex Smith's *XR6* and Don Tognotti´s *King T*. In 1988 Winfield was honored with the

Not all 1949-51 Mercurys were chopped when they were customized. Bill Wolf took his '51 to Winfield for a mild modification. the front fenders were given Buick headlights, and a new grille was made from tubing. Lake pipes and Buick side trim dressed up the lowered Merc after it was painted in a bronze-colored candy paint. *Gene Winfield*

Car Builder of the Year award at the Oakland show. He can't even count how many times his paint jobs have won best paint at different shows.

Today, he spends most of his time at the shop building cars for different customers, when he is not at any of the bigger custom events on the West Coast selling his stuff. He is also a "hired gun" who comes to the customer to paint a car, using a local paint booth in their hometown. Top customizers in Northern California, like John D'Agostino, Richard Zocchi, and others have used this paint service. It does not look like Winfield will slow down very much in the near future, so we might just be able to see his fabulous paint jobs and custom car creations for a long time to come.

Larry Watson

The first time I saw a Larry Watson–style paint job was in the late 1950s in my hometown of Stockholm, when the local custom king Bo Sandberg customized a '55 Mercury. He painted it with panels in white, gold, and turquoise. It was something that I had never seen before, and the paint made the car into something very special. After that day, I soon discovered that it was the crazy California-based paint king Larry Watson who had inspired Bo Sandberg. I followed the rod and custom scene in the magazines and read everything I could find about Watson and the other customizers.

Watson began in the mid-1950s doing pinstriping on his friends' cars in the driveway of his parents' house in Bellflower, California. His inspiration came from seeing Dean Jefferies pinstripe a chopped Merc. The first pinstriping he did was on his own custom '50 Chevy. His friends at Bellflower High thought Watson had it done by Von Dutch, because he was the only pinstriper they knew about.

Watson's first real customer was Harvey Budhoff, who had a lavender customized '50 Ford. It was a simple, basic white pinstripe job. After the other guys at the local drive-in saw Budhoff's shoebox Ford, there was a group of them waiting

Larry Watson's '50 Chevy was named *Grapevine*. It was nosed and decked and lowered and had some mild modifications done to it, including '54 Merc taillights and a Chevy "teeth-grille." The girl posing was Watson's girlfriend, Elaine Sterling. *Jim Potter*

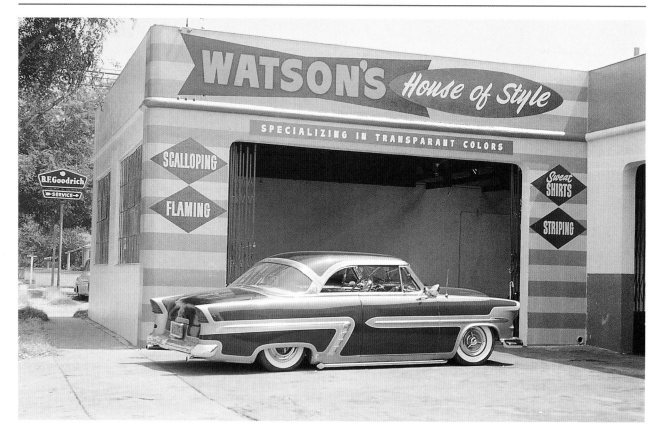

This picture was taken at Watson's first shop on Bellflower Boulevard, Long Beach, in 1958. The car is Ray Moore's '52 Ford. It was de-chromed and lowered and had frenched headlights and custom taillights installed, after which it was panel-painted in burgundy on gold. *Jim Potter*

Here is Larry Watson posing with his '58 Thunderbird in 1958. This was the car that would get him into more magazines than any other custom he ever painted. The panel-paint job became part of his trademark, and here the T-Bird had been painted with faded panels-in-panels. *Jim Potter*

in Watson's driveway when he returned from school the next day. After doing pinstriping on many local cars, some customers wanted him to do more than just striping. From then on, it was all kinds of things such as eyeballs, roses, and so on, and Watson became well known at the local drive-ins.

"Scalloping" was something Watson came up with when he had to cover up some paint runs a local body shop had done on a '54 Chevy. He rented a spray gun and compressor, then taped up some scallops on the hood and the trunk. With those scallops, Watson created something much bigger than he could have dreamed of. One of his early customers was Duane Steck, who owned the chopped '53 Chevy *Moonglow*. "When that car showed up at the Bellflower Clock drive-in, all the boys wanted scallops on their cars," recalls Watson. It soon became a problem to paint cars on the driveway of his parents' home, so Watson decided to look for a location to set up

One of the first full flame-jobs Watson did was on Al Lazarus' '55 Chevy hardtop. He created a new style of long-lick flames he called "seaweed-flames" after somebody pointed out that they looked like seaweed. He traced the flames from one side to the other to get them the same and save many hours of work. The owner, Al Lazarus, and Watson are still friends today.
Jim Potter

shop. At the time, business was booming for the custom car builders and painters in the south Los Angeles area. Some people feel that the real custom car era was between 1945 and 1955, right after the boys came home from the war. It is quite likely that the evolution was from the early customs with a lot of modifications and metalwork, to the semi-customs, which were just restyled cars with pretty paint jobs.

In the late 1950s and early 1960s, the Detroit cars were nearly customs straight from the factory, which made a big difference for the boys at the local drive-ins. Even 16- and 17-year-old owners of brand-new cars had them restyled and custom painted in the late 1950s. It was also a new category of wild, purpose-built show cars. Wild bubble-top cars from guys like "Big Daddy" Roth, Darryl Starbird, and Bill Cushenberry were touring the shows all over the country in the early 1960s. People wanted to see something wild at the shows, and those guys gave them plenty of it.

Watson is quick to point out that the high point of the custom car era was in the early-to-late 1950s which includes most of the new tricks in paint jobs that he and others introduced. Everything from pin striping to flames, scallops, and panel-in-panel paint in candy and pearls became really popular during this period, so one could agree with Watson. Dean Jefferies, Von Dutch, and George Barris were a few of the people in the area who were involved at this time.

After Watson opened his "House of Style" paint shop on Bellflower Boulevard in Long Beach in 1956, he got plenty of coverage from the custom car magazines. He was just out of school and fast becoming the king of custom paint. Full paint jobs in metallics, candies, and pearls were soon on the program.

Flames were also something Watson mastered early on, inspired by Von Dutch and Dean Jefferies. Two of the cars that people remember from those days are Al Lazarus' black '55 Chevy with

This group shot, taken in 1957, shows six of the Watson-painted semi-customs. The best known is Jack James's '57 Buick in the foreground, which was given the full flame treatment by Watson. The painter himself is sitting right in the middle, and you can also see that most of the car owners were young guys. *Jim Potter*

In 1959 Watson bought this brand-new '59 Caddy Coupe and had Bill DeCarr restyle it by de-chroming, nosing, decking, and lowering it. He also installed solenoids to open the doors. After the success with the previous '58 T-Bird's panel-paint job, he stayed with the same concept and painted it in a deep burgundy candy on a brilliant white pearl base. *Jim Potter*

silver-green flames all over it, and Jack James' '57 Buick in black with yellow and orange flames. The '55 Chevy was lowered and had the door handles removed and the stock grille replaced before Watson painted it. James' Buick was done in late 1956, so it was a new car that Watson totally covered in flames. It may be the best-known flamed custom ever. "Jack James was sponsored by a local Buick dealer and he wanted his car flamed all the way to the back bumper," recalls Watson. "Three of my pals helped out with sanding after I laid out the flames, and to save time I traced the first side on tissue paper over to the other side. When the yellow and orange was sprayed in enamel, I used a trick to rub out the edges with chrome polish.

A normal flame job over the hood and front fenders was about 35 bucks, so for James' Buick I charged him 65 bucks, because it was so much more work."

When it came to his own custom cars, Watson had his '50 Chevy *Grapevine*, built by Ed Shelhaas. "I didn't paint that car first time around," Watson confesses, "even if most people

NEXT PAGE: Some of Watson's customers came from out of town with their cars, and 15-year-old Floyd DeBore was one of them, with his new '58 Pontiac Bonneville. The Pontiac was given a mild modification and a lowering before Watson painted it in different shades of gold, red, and brown, with panels, flames, and pinstriping. *Jim Potter*

Duane Steck's '53 Chevy custom *Moonglow* has been many early Chevy custom lovers' favorite car through the years. Watson first did some pinstriping around pictures of a couple of nude ladies on the hood. A year later, when the car had some additional work done and was repainted, he did the white scallops. Here, the top is chopped, the headlights are frenched, and the rear fenders are extended with new taillights. *Jim Potter*

Different kinds of flames and scallops were what the customers wanted before 1958, when Watson came up with the panel-paint. In this photo we can see Jack Arnold's '56 Merc in white with scallops, Downey Benny's '58 Chevy with flames, and John Bussman's '56 Chevy with flames. *Jim Potter*

thought so." Later he repainted it in a lavender pearl with silver scallops. He was 19 years old when he sold *Grapevine* in 1957 for $1,500, in order to buy something new. He checked out the dealers and all the new cars, but the car he wanted was an exclusive Cadillac Brougham, which was way too expensive for him. After looking at the Fords in Downey, he found out that the forthcoming '58 T-Bird would make a good custom. He didn't know it at the time, but this was the car that was going to give him more publicity than any other.

At the point when he picked up the new T-Bird from the dealer, Watson had his shop in one of the buildings next to Barris. Bill Hines and Bill DeCarr over at Barris did the bodywork, including filling the holes for the door handles and chrome trim. The car was also lowered before Watson painted it. "That was the first car I did panel paint on," Watson recalls, "and I will never forget the first time I drove it to Harvey's Broiler. The girls were screaming and whistling, I barely had time to open the door before they got in the car." It was the first time he mixed a candy burgundy with a silver pearl base and did paneling that followed the lines of the car. Later it was repainted with more panels-in-panels plus more pinstriping.

Gary Niemo, the current owner, recently restored this car, and Watson helped the owner match the paint and outline the panels, using pictures from 1958 as references. Part of Watson's popularity was his use of brilliant colors. "I liked to mix up new colors all the time," he says, "and my customers were nice enough to let me try things." In those days, Watson and his helpers—sometimes as many as five or six at a time—worked grueling 12-hour days, seven days a week. They pumped out custom paint jobs, many of them on nearly brand-new cars.

In 1959 it was time for Watson to build a new custom. He bought a brand-new '59 Cadillac Coupe (not the Coupe DeVille, but the regular 62 series, which he liked better, thanks to the tuck and roll-looking interior it came with). He drove the new car straight to Bill DeCarr to have it nosed and decked, the door handles removed, and solenoids installed. The springs were also cut all around to lower the car before it was painted. When it was

Larry Watson today, again posing with the now restored '58 Thunderbird that gave him much of the fame he received after it was built and painted. It was built very quickly in late 1957, as soon as he took delivery of it from the Ford dealer. Today the T-Bird is a very mild custom, but it is easy to understand that it must have been extreme to see at the local drive-in in the fall of 1957.

The car that made the most commotion of all was this '58 T-Bird that Watson bought brand new and modified in three short weeks, to make it to a custom show in L.A. Its bodywork was done at Barris' shop, were Bill DeCarr and Bill Hines removed all chrome trim, lowered it, and installed side pipes on it. Finally, it received the first panel-paint job done by Watson. *Jim Potter*

George Mitobe's '57 Ranchero was given a combination of scallops/panel and flame paint job in gold and green candy. Just like on his own '59 Caddy, Watson used chrome tape on the top and around the windows, which were covered with clear. The Ranchero was given a mild custom job with lowering a new grill, louvers in the hood, sidepipes, and custom hubcaps. The interior was updated with a white tuck and roll. *Jim Potter*

The '58 Bird is now owned by Gary Niemo, and it has been restored with all the original equipment intact. Watson helped out by laying out the panels, mixing the paint, and pinstriping around the paneling. With the help of old photos, the paint is just as it was in 1958. This Ford was modified even before people knew what a '58 T-Bird looked like, and the boys at the George Barris shop helped out with the bodywork. The emblems, chrome trim, and handles were shaved off of the body and all the holes filled before Watson painted it. Lake pipes and Appleton spotlights were details that most customizers used on their cars in those days.

Jack James brought his brand-new '57 Buick to Larry Watson to have it flamed, all over too, not just the nose. Watson gave it the full treatment, and with help from three of his friends to sand it down, the job was done in one day. He charged James 65 bucks for it, because it was a lot more work than a regular flame job. James was sponsored by a local Buick dealer and later the car got many people to come in and take a closer look at the new model. *Jim Potter*

back at the Watson shop, he mixed a special ruby candy that was applied over a super-brilliant white pearl. He also used the panel paint style on the '59. He then came up with another new concept by using 1/4-inch-wide chrome tape stripes on top of the car, which were covered with many layers of clear finish. Watson drove his '59 Caddy for a year before he traded it for the car he really wanted, a '57 Caddy Brougham.

By 1959 the magazines were full of Watson-painted customs, and his T-Bird had been picked as one of the top 10 in *Custom Cars Annual*. He was definately one of the most productive and cool guys of California customizing, and is considered a legend.

In the mid-1970s, he painted a lot of vans and other full-size cars. Though a visit to his shop would have revealed that not so many traditional custom paint jobs were completed at this time, he still turned out some very nice results. Even today, more than 45 years after he got started, you can hear customizers use expressions like "a Watson-style custom," "Watson scallops," "Watson paneling," or "Watson flames." Without a doubt, Larry Watson has given the custom car scene many good ideas.

John D'Agostino

orn in Pittsburg, California, in 1950, John D'Agostino got into building and customizing model cars when he was a child. D'Agostino was lucky because his hometown of Pittsburg and nearby Antioch were hot spots for custom cars when he grew up. Cars built by the best in the business turned up at the local Hazel's drive-in through the 1950s and 1960s, so he was definitely in the right spot at the right time. Frank DeRosa was one of the popular local customizers who had done work for people in the area for some years.

D'Agostino's first custom was a '56 Chevy hardtop that was lowered, molded, and painted in a two-tone Royal Triton purple and white by DeRosa. D'Agostino was driving his custom to high school and showing it at local shows. When D'Agostino attended college in Phoenix, Arizona, he drove a mildly customized pearl white and gold '63 Pontiac Grand Prix, cruising the streets with cool tunes spun on his 45-rpm record player, which was installed in the car.

Just before leaving college, however, D'Agostino ordered a brand-new '70 Pontiac Grand Prix and

One of the most award-winning cars through the years has been the '53 Caddy *Marilyn*. The car was built by John Aiello at Acme Customs in Antioch and was shown for the first time in 1998 at the Oakland Show. It won the World's Most Beautiful Custom and Goodguys' Custom d'Elegance of the Year.

It was in 1973, after John D'Agostino saw *American Graffiti*, that he got into Mercurys and built the *Midnight Sensation*. It was chopped by Rod Powell and lowered by Bill Hines in L.A. *John D'Agostino*

In 1982 D'Agostino bought this '58 Chrysler named *Golden Sunrise* from his friend, Rich Zocchi. It was built by Gene Winfield and had one of his blended candy paint jobs, wire wheels, custom grille, and a pearl white interior. *John D'Agostino*

took it straight to Art Himsl in Concord, California, to be customized. It was first shown at the '70 Oakland Roadster Show, where it won "Outstanding Custom." The car was lowered, molded, and painted different shades of candy gold and tangerine. Even in those early days, this car had D'Agostino's trademark chromed wire wheels. He showed the Pontiac at all the ISCA shows on the West Coast during 1970 and 1971 (about 14 shows in all).

After owning two older-style customs, one '49 Olds Coupe by DeRosa and a '60 Buick by Himsl, D'Agostino got another new car, this time a '72 Buick Riviera "Boattail" that he took to Himsl for some wild customizing. "This time, I had a top designer sketch the car for me, before we got started," says D'Agostino. Among the modifications were the grille, headlights, taillights, and the wheelwells, which were radius-flared. Art Himsl and Mike Haas also painted the Buick in red metalflake toned to different shades of tangerine with silver scallops. It was awarded "International Class Champion" in the full custom category in the 1972–73 season. "I can remember when we took some pictures in front of the Buick with me, Rich Zocchi, and Reggie Jackson at the San Mateo show that year" says D'Agostino. "The late 1960s and early 1970s were low on customs, and Zocchi had taken a layoff from building any new customs until 1973 when we showed two Lincolns together at the San Francisco Cow Palace. Zocchi had a mild '56 Mark II in black pearl, and mine was a wilder '72 Mark IV that was built at Himsl's Paint Studios in Concord, California." This was the first time D'Agostino and Zocchi showed their customs together side by side, which continues today a quarter of a century later. The Lincoln was sold right out of the Oakland show to a Lincoln dealer in San Francisco.

In the summer of 1973, D'Agostino spent some time with Bill Hines and his son Mike in Los Angeles. One night they took D'Agostino to see the movie *American Graffiti*. "I immediately wanted a custom '51 Mercury," he says. He found one nearly restored in nearby

The *Royal Tahitian* was a '53 Mercury that D'Agostino had Bill Reasoner build for him in 1986. Reasoner painted it in red candy, and it won a bunch of big trophies before John traded it for the Winfield-built *Jade Idol* in 1987.
John D'Agostino

The *Starfire* was a '57 Cadillac Eldorado that John had built by Farello's Kustom Kreations in Reno, Nevada. Bill Hines did the finish work in lead before he painted it in candy apple red.

Eddie Martinez stitched the pearl white tuck and roll interior of the Cadillac. The *Starfire* won many awards, including Best of Show at the 1993 Paso Robles show. It was also chosen to be part of Mattel's "Legends" series of model cars.

Concord, but the car was so nice that he simply finished the restoration and showed it for the first time at the 1973 Santa Rosa Autorama. He decided to buy another Mercury to customize; this one was owned by a fireman in Castro Valley and would later become the *Midnight Sensation*. D'Agostino took that Merc to Rod Powell's shop in Salinas, California, for a top chop—the first such surgery on a Merc that was done at Powell's. Next, D'Agostino took the Merc to Bill Hines' shop in Bellflower, California, for a lowering job. At the shop he decided to have some additional customizing work done, including the installation of a '54 Pontiac grille, '52 Lincoln taillights, and '53 Buick teardrop headlights. "With all the work done and the car in white primer," D'Agostino recalls, "I remember cruising down to the parking lot at the 1975 Oakland Roadster Show, then finding the car surrounded by people." Chopped Mercs were very rare to see at the time. The car was garaged and later sold to Harry Craycroft, who never finished it either, but he took it to Powell's and had the fade-aways done

The *Starfire* was chopped by Farello's Kustom Kreations, and both the front and rear ends were given modifications. The "wings" were extended and the taillights were changed for two pairs of '59 Cadillac "bullets."

The beautiful *Emperor* was teamed up with a '60s-style semi-custom-built '61 Oldsmobile called *Golden Starfire*. Both of the cars were driven to the 1995 Paso Robles Show, where they won top awards. Whitewalls and chromed wire wheels were becoming a trademark for D'Agostino.

on it. The flathead was replaced by a 351 Ford Cleveland engine and drivetrain combination.

After the '82 Oakland show, D'Agostino bought the Winfield-built '58 Chrysler *Golden Sunrise* from his friend Rich Zocchi. "It just happened that I traded the Chrysler to Harry later for my old Merc," he says. The *Midnight Sensation* was taken back to Powell's again to be completed and painted. With a lavender pearl paint job and a new Kenny Foster interior, it finally made its debut at the November 1983 San Francisco *Rod & Custom* show. Later, at the '84 Oakland show, the *Midnight Sensation* won several top awards, including the Sam Barris Memorial Award.

D'Agostino's next custom, which was also a hit on the show circuit, was a Bill Reasoner–built '53 Merc named *The Royal Tahitian*. It was a mild custom with a candy red paint job, and it won "Best of Show" at the popular West Coast Customs Paso Robles show in 1986. D'Agostino

Even the interior of the *Emperor* was made in extra-deluxe and concept style. Sahagon Custom Car Concepts in Concord did the interior in mint leatherette, English tweed, and Italian emerald velvet. D'Agostino didn't stop there—he also installed a TV and VCR in the console between the custom seats.

In 1995 D'Agostino built two new customs, and the most impressive was this '57 Lincoln called the *Royal Emperor*. The car was built by John Aiello and Darryl Hollenbeck to be more of a '50s concept car than a custom car. The lines of the *Emperor* are very impressive, and people didn't understand how D'Agostino could turn the front wheels enough to go around a

corner. The Lincoln was seemingly made to be a custom car, and with the new lines and a green faded candy paint job by the master, Gene Winfield, it became something very special. The inspiration came from some drawings done by Thom Taylor. The top was more or less a back-to-front piece, even if Aiello and Hollenbeck made a new one.

showed it at the '87 Sacramento Autorama before trading it for the Gene Winfield–built *Jade Idol.* "We traded right after the awards ceremony at the show," says D'Agostino, "and it was a child-hood dream to drive the *Idol* home that foggy Sunday night. I could not wait to call Winfield Monday morning about it." The plan was to have Winfield redo the car like it was when he built it in the late '50s. D'Agostino never got around to doing that, because he was building his next big winner at the time, a '40 Merc Coupe called *Stardust,* that was modified and painted by Bill Reasoner. The *Jade Idol* was later sold to a guy back East, where it remains today.

Stardust made its debut at the 1988 Oakland show and went on to win many awards, including Best of Show at the Paso Robles Show and the Sam Barris Memorial Award at Oakland. It eventually ended up at Harrah's Museum in Reno, Nevada, where it was displayed for a few years before it was sold. It was last seen at the "Men and Machines" exhibition at the Oakland Museum in 1996.

The next D'Agostino winner at Oakland was a '56 Lincoln built by Winfield and Reasoner called *The Royal Empress.* This won the Al Slonaker Award at the 1991 Oakland show and was chosen for the Harry Bradley Design Achievement Award at the Leadsled Spectacular the same year. Bill Abate of New Jersey now owns the Lincoln. In 1993, D'Agostino debuted the '57 Cadillac Eldorado *Starfire* at the Oakland show. John first took it to Farcello's Kustom creations in Reno, Nevada, to have it chopped and then Bill Hines finished it in lead before he painted it in the fabulous candy apple red. The interior was a pearl white Eddie Martinez tuck and roll. The *Starfire* won Best of Show at the 1993 Paso Robles show and was chosen by Mattel for the signature series of Hot Wheels.

In 1995, D'Agostino had two new customs built for the show circuit. John Aiello and Darryl Hollenbeck in Antioch, California, built the '57 Lincoln *Royal Emperor*, painted by Gene Winfield. The car won the Sam Barris Award that year and "Best of Show" at the Paso Robles show. The *Emperor* was sent on a Northern European tour the following year. The second custom was a '61 Olds, *Golden Starfire*, which was a mildly customized vehicle in early '60s style and painted in

This '61 Olds Super 88 was called *Golden Starfire* and was built by John Aiello, who lowered it by cutting the coils. In addition, he C-ed the frame in the rear. The body was stripped of all chrome, nosed, decked, and molded before it was painted in Pagan Gold candy by Darryl Hollenbeck.

The "bubbletop" of the 1961 GM models is a very special car for customizers, and it was a good choice for D'Agostino as a semi-custom. The rear of the Olds is different from the Chevy and Pontiac, but the large taillights and the rocket-shaped rear fenders go well with the Olds style.

The pearl white Naugahyde interior of the *Golden Starfire* was installed over two '63 Buick Riviera seats by Sahagons Custom Car Concepts. A '60s-style V-shape tuck and roll was done to get a more time-perfect custom look. A sharp eye can also see that D'Agostino didn't install only a TV in the console, but also an old style 45-rpm record-player.

PREVIOUS PAGE: In 1997 D'Agostino was back with two new customs. The first of them was a '57 Chrysler Imperial called *Imperial Royal*. The Acme Custom Team in Antioch, California, built the car, and master painter Gene Winfield finished it. The top was chopped and the body was modified all around. Both front and rear were customized and the suspension was lowered.

The most impressive engine in any of D'Agostino's customs is the 392 hemi in the *Imperial Royal*. The mega-big hemi was rebuilt and detailed down to the last part. Not many custom builders go through the detailing with their engines like D'Agostino did on the hemi.

D'Agostino wanted the interior of the *Imperial* to be in late '50s- early '60s-style, and Sahagons did a good job with the swivel seats and the pearl white naugahyde/orange tweed. In real 1950s style, a console was created for a TV and a stereo system.

a gold candy color. 1997 was a repeat of 1995, with two more customs built. This time a radical "concept style" '57 Chrysler Imperial called the *Imperial Royal* with Acme in Antioch and Gene Winfield teaming up to build a new winner. It won the Harry Bradley Design Achievement Award at the Sacramento Autorama in 1997, as well as the Goodguys Custom d'Elegance of the Year award. Shown along with the *Imperial* at the Sacramento Autorama was a chopped '61 Thunderbird in candy apple red with gold scallops. This T-Bird, named *Firestar*, was built at the Lucky Seven Custom Shop in Antioch. Right after the Sacramento show, the T-Bird was shipped to Europe and Sweden, where it went on a show tour.

1998 brought two more Cadillac customs, and the *Marilyn* was a '53 Coupe DeVille with a chopped Carson top built by John Aiello. It was painted light yellow pearl with golden highlights. This Caddy won many awards including World's Most Beautiful Custom at the 1998 Sacramento show, as well as First in Class at Oakland, Sacramento, and Portland, and best paint and interior at many of the shows. The *Marilyn* was sold to an Australian at the Pebble Beach Auction in 1999 for $125,000. The second Cadillac that year was a '57 Biaritz that was named *Cool '57*. The car was first customized by Gene Winfield but was never finished, so D'Agostino bought it and took it to the Acme boys in Antioch. Darryl Hollenbeck painted the Caddy in a House of Kolor candy raspberry red, and Contra Costa Vinyl in Pittsburg finished it off with a pearl-white interior in Swedish Elmo Leather. This Caddy also won its share of awards.

For the 1999 show season John D'Agostino was back to a Lincoln again with a full-size '58 Continental customized by John Aiello at Acme Custom Cars in Antioch. During the last few years, air-ride suspension has been a part of customizing, and John was one of the first to install it on his customs. This new Lincoln made its

Together with the '57 *Imperial*, this '61 T-Bird was built in 1997. D'Agostino named the T-Bird *Firestar*, and it was built at the Lucky Seven Shop in Antioch. The suspension was dropped and air-ride made it possible to adjust the height between 4 and 5 inches. Wince Burne chopped the top, cleaned the body of all chrome, rounded the door corners, and created a new hood scoop. Just before the car was shipped off on its European tour, these pictures were taken in D'Agostino's hometown of Antioch. This is his favorite picture, with the palm tree. The T-Bird, with its candy apple red paint with gold scallops, was a show winner on the tour.

The body modifications on the *Marilyn* were done by John Aiello, who also made the new Carson-type top for it after chopping the windshield. The body was given fade-away fenders, scoops, extended tailfins, a frenched grille, and a modified continental kit. It was painted by Darryll Hollenbeck in a custom mix of ivory and gold candy/pearl. It was later sold at the Pebble Beach auction for $125,000 to an Australian.

INSET: Craig Willits upholstered the interior of the *Marilyn* in pearl white Swedish Elmo leather, and the dash was painted in candy with the instrumentation and the column re-chromed by Sherm's Custom Plating in Sacramento.

How low can you go? The super clean T-Bird is dropped to a maximum. The "wings" were modified and so were the taillights. The whitewalls and chromed wire wheels are a part of D'Agostino's trademark.

The *Cool '57* was built at the same time as the *Marilyn* as a joint venture between D'Agostino and A&A. It was built in just 87 days, but was started in the 1970s by Gene Winfield and Rod Powell for a Hollywood movie producer.
As with so many of his customs before, the *Cool '57* was also modified by John Aiello at Acme Customs and painted in raspberry/magenta candy by Darryl Hollenbeck. Gregg Philbrick and Ken Whisler on Contra Costa stitched the white Swedish Elmo leather interior vinyl in Pittsburg.

For 1999, John had a full-size '58 Lincoln built that made its debut at the Oakland show. The same team at Acme Customs did most of the work. John Aiello made all of the body modifications and installed the air suspension. Darryl Hollenbeck painted it in a light blue pearl. Bob Divine did the pearl white interior.

debut at the 50th Grand National Roadster Show in San Francisco and won him plenty of awards. For the 2000 Oakland show, D'Agostino introduced two more Cadillacs, with a '54 Coupe DeVille as his own new car. Again it was built by Aiello, and the two legends, Gene Winfield and Frank DeRosa, painted the Caddy in a color-shifting gold candy color. The second Caddy was a project called *The*

Cadster, and was built and painted by Frank DeRosa. It started out as a '59 Caddy Coupe De-Ville but it is now a wild two-seated roadster with a shorter wheel base and a chopped windshield. D'Agostino has new custom car plans going on in his head at all times, so I'll bet we will see some new wild projects in the years to come at the Grand National Roadster Show in San Francisco.

Chapter 4

Rick Dore

Rick was born in the 1950s in New York, and the first custom he got close to was in the early 1960s when a friend of his family had a chopped shoebox '50 Ford—a very exciting thing to see. In the 1970s, many of his friends bought brand-new muscle cars when they came home from Vietnam. "I thought the muscle cars were very cool," Dore remembers, "but my love was for the customs, even in the early days." One day in the 1980s, when he was sitting at a red light, a chopped '51 Merc pulled up alongside his car. "That ignited my passion for customs again," says Dore. He was now in a financial position that made it possible for him to afford to build a custom too.

Dore's first custom was a '57 Buick named *Lavender Persuasion* and built by Squeeg's Customs in Arizona. The top was chopped 3 inches and both the front and rear fenders were extended with custom headlights and taillights. To give the car a nice ride, Dore had the frame cut by the firewall and a Nova clip installed. The two-tone lavender candy-pearl paint made the car stand out at the Oakland show, where it was first shown in 1993. It was a big thrill for Dore to enter this show with his first real custom. After that,

Rick Dore's dropped and chopped Buick received a Chevy Nova frontclip, plus a Chevy 350 engine/transmission combination. The top was chopped 3 inches and the fenders extended with Packard taillights in the rear. The two-tone candy/pearl Lavender paint job was completed by Squeeg's Customs.

Rick completed most of his work on the first real custom he built, this '57 Buick, at Squeeg's Customs in Mesa, Arizona. Rick's wife, Susan, gets involved with the cars by working with style and colors.

Dore went straight back to the drawing board to come up with the next winner. In the meantime, he was driving the '57 Buick to different events and entering other shows like the big Paso Robles custom show in late May, which is a very good place to get some new ideas.

Dore's second big winner was a '53 Buick Riviera called *Breathless*. With its deep purple paint job and smooth body lines, it was something very special. "It was my wife Susan who liked the body style and talked me into getting the '53 for our next project," says Dore. He got plenty of help

with the Buick from two of his big heroes: Dick Dean and Bill Reasoner. Dean chopped the windshield and built the Carson-style top, while Reasoner in northern California did more than 25 body modifications, including frenching and peaking the headlights 3 inches, and adding a '49 Buick trunk lid, handmade taillights, and a frenched rear bumper. Reasoner also painted the car in a black pearl base with a few topcoats of candy purple. But before all that was done, Dore took the Buick to Route 66 Rod & Custom shop in Albuquerque, New Mexico, to get it subframed with a Chevy Nova front clip and rear end. It took Dore 54 weeks to build the new custom, and it was a real winner. The car was finished in mid-January 1995, just in time for the Oakland show where it won First in Class Next, he took it to the Sacramento Show, and was stunned when he was presented with World's Most Beautiful Custom award for *Breathless*.

By now, Dore was a well-known name at all the custom shops on the West Coast, which made it easier for him to get work done on his cars and still keep deadlines. "People ask me a lot about how I can get my cars built so quick," says Dore, "and it all comes down to knowing what you want and getting good help from the right professionals."

Dore knew he was onto a new winner when he found a '49 Caddy fastback that had been parked in a barn since 1958. The smooth, long lines of the fastback were made even better by a Bill Reasoner chopped top, 4 inches in the front and 5 inches in the rear. Bill did all the rest of the bodywork, with all chrome trim shaved off, headlights frenched, and so forth, before he painted it in a toned candy Tequila Sunrise (orange). The suspension was lowered, with dropped front spindles and a set of Unkl Al's lowglide springs. Dore then used a lot of late 1960s and early 1970s Caddy parts to get it updated in the motor, transmission, brakes, and steering departments. The Caddy was called *Majestic* and it looked like a King's Caddy when it was first rolled in at the Oakland show in 1996. It won numerous awards during the season, before it was sold to a buyer on the East Coast about a year later.

Dore got an even bigger response from his next car, a '36 Ford. Dore wanted to build an old Westergard-style '36 custom, but the problem was to find a good car for the project. Dore's friend, Unkl Al, called him one day with a '36 Ford coupe for sale. A roadster would have been optimal, but the next best was a coupe. Dore went to Oregon to look at the car and found that both the body and frame were good enough for his project.

Unkl Al started with giving the chassis a Mustang II–type front end and a nine-inch Ford rear end. Air-ride suspension and brackets for a 350/350 Chevy motor-trans combination got the rolling chassis ready. Acme Custom Cars in Antioch,

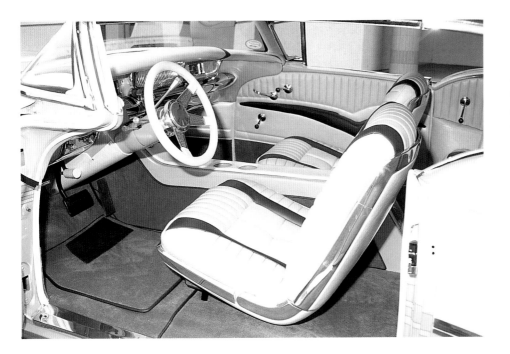

Rick wanted a high-quality interior inside the Buick to match the paint job, so he took it to Eddie Salcido in Tucson, Arizona. The seats for the Buick came out of a T-Bird and then were reupholstered with white and wine-red leather.

NEXT PAGE: *Breathless* was just that. Rick started with a '53 Buick Super Riviera, on Susan's recommendations. Dick Dean chopped the windshield and built a Carson-type top for it. The frame's front clip came from a '75 Chevy Nova plus a rear end from the same car at the Route 66 Rod & Customs shop. Bill Reasoner in northern California did all the bodywork with 25 different modifications and painted it.

ABOVE: Some of the handy work of bodyman Bill Reasoner can be seen in this picture; the rear fenders were completely reworked and given handformed taillights. The bumper in the rear is the front bumper from a '56 Plymouth.

LEFT: The interior of the *Breathless* was covered in white pearl leather and lavender fabric. Eddie Salcido handmade all the panels and consoles before he upholstered the Chevy Monte Carlo seats plus the handmade rear seat.

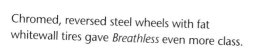

Chromed, reversed steel wheels with fat whitewall tires gave *Breathless* even more class.

Another great winner was the '49 Caddy Sedanette Fastback that Rick built in 1995. The supersmooth lines of the Caddy were improved by Bill Reasoner with a 4 -inch chop of the top and by shaving all the chrome and handles off the body.

California—and that means John Aiello and painter Darryl Hollenbeck—did all the bodywork.

While the the bodywork was being done, Dore got on the plane from his hometown in Arizona to overlook the work at Acme once a week. He also helped Aiello to design the shape of the Carson-type top before it was covered with sheet metal. When the car was ready to be painted, he and Hollenbeck took a full night with test-spraying panels to get the exact right mix for the '36. The car was built in only nine months and was a big success when it was shown at the Oakland show, where it won Best Custom. In Sacramento it won its class and the Joe Bailon Award. The third show was the Goodguys event, where Dore received the Custom D'Eleganze and the America's Most Beautiful Custom awards. Pictures of the '36 custom with the Packard grille have been published all over the world and shown at the big events, including the SEMA show in Las Vegas.

After Dore's great success with his '36 Ford, it was not easy for him to follow up with another winner. During the planning of the next custom

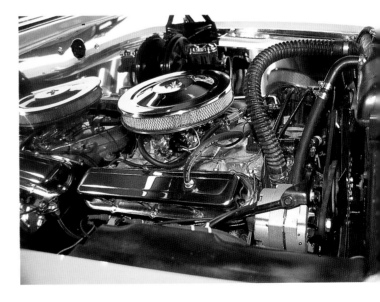

In the *Majestic* Caddy, Rick used a big-block '68 Caddy motor that was rebuilt by Desert Cylinders in Phoenix, Arizona. Rick likes to do a great deal of detailing work under the hood on his customs and the Caddy had an assortment of shiny parts around the engine.

Bill Reasoner did a lot of bodywork on the Caddy, including frenching the headlights in the front fenders, frenching the grille, and cleaning up the bumper. Bill also painted the *Majestic* in Tequila Sunrise orange candy from House of Color.

The unreal lines of the rear of the '36 gives us a look at what Westergard and others were building in the late '40s and early '50s. Rick had John Aiello at Acme Custom Cars in Antioch, California, do the bodywork, with widened and extended '39 Lincoln Zephyr rear fenders. The top was cut off the coupe body and replaced by a Carson-style hardtop.

The most published of Rick's customs has been the '36 Ford in Westergard style that was built in '96–'97, and presented at the Oakland show in January, 1998. It all began when Rick's friend Unkl Al found this '36 Ford Coupe for sale in Oregon. Before Dore picked it up, he had Unkl Al install a Mustang II-type front end. Combined with Air Ride suspension in each corner, the Ford can easily lower and raise between 4 and 5 inches.

for the 2000 season, he was approached by his friend, Don Makofske, in Pennsylvania, who wanted his help to build a high-dollar '56 Lincoln custom coupe. Dore knew that he could build the two cars at the same time, with some good planning. He used more money than planned on to start with the best available car, but Dore was quickly compensated with fewer working hours and less bodywork.

The 1956 Mark III Lincoln cost $13,500, but Dore and Makofske also got a very good, straight, and nice car to start with. Dore's own car was already in the works, a '62 Thunderbird, which he took to Squegs in Mesa, Arizona. The T-Bird was chopped and the wheelwells and the front and rear sheetmetal were modified. The chassis was modified with Fatman dropped spindles and Unkl Al's rear springs, plus an Air-Ride Technologies airbag system in all four corners. When the bodywork was done, it was painted in House of Kolors Sunrise candy orange by Squeg's son, Doug Jerger. At the same time the T-Bird was built at Squegs in Arizona, the Lincoln was built by Darryl Hollenbeck in Concord, California. The

The interior was done by Craig Willits in pearl white leather, the seat was based on a Glide Engineering seat, and the door panels were handmade before being upholstered. The steering column came out of a Dodge Van with a LeCarra steering wheel on top of it.

Rick thought that a LaSalle grille would be something that many customizers would choose, so he wanted something else, and that was a '40 Packard grille. The front end also got a pair of '37 Buick headlights welded on to the fenders.

Don and Rick wanted some extra power for the big Lincoln Coupe, so a brand new-454 Chevy big-block crate motor and a T.H. 400 transmission were dropped into the car. Rick is well known for his detailing, which can be seen here under the hood of the Lincoln, with the firewall and inner fenders all smoothed out.

This Mark II Lincoln was built for Rick's friend Don Makofske in Pennsylvania and Rick was the one to organize it, as if it were just his own car. Darryl Hollenbeck in Concord, California did all the bodywork and paint. The top was chopped 3 inches and the body was modified, front and rear.

The rear of the Lincoln was modified with a sunken bumper, the Lincoln trade mark Continental kit was sectioned a few inches, and the rear panel rounded with the license plate sunken.

Rick's latest winner is this '63 Ford Thunderbird that he first showed off at the 1999 SEMA Show in Las Vegas, and then at the Oakland Roadster Show in California. The top was chopped 3 inches and the rear quarter panels stretched, plus the wheel wells were modified.

The rear of the T-Bird had the bumper shaved off and replaced by a rolled panel. The trunk had the corners rounded and the special exhausts were frenched into the body together with the license plate. Special, custom-made taillights were sunk in the rear fenders. The T-Bird was a class winner at the Oakland Show in 2000.

top was chopped on the Lincoln, too, and Hollenbeck performed numerous body modifications. Door corners were rounded off, front and rear fenders extended, headlights frenched, a new grille made, and the rear had the Continental kit cut down a couple of inches to smooth out the lines, then the bumpers were sunk into the bodywork, both front and rear. Hollenbeck also painted the Lincoln in an ice-blue mix of pearls and candies. The chassis had an air-ride system installed, and for power a

new 454 big-block Chevy with a T.H.400 transmission was dropped in the engine bay. Dore's good eye for detail paid off when both the cars were ready to go to the Oakland Roadster Show. Both new cars gave Dore plenty of ink in the magazines and many trophies, including Best in Class for both cars at the Oakland show. Dore has not even been an active custom car creator for 10 years, but he is still a well-known winner of the big awards on the West Coast show circuit.

Jimmie Vaughan

Jimmie Vaughan is not only a famous rock and blues guitar player (the brother of the late Stevie Ray Vaughan and earlier playing with the Fabulous Thunderbirds), but also a custom car creator with roots and dream cars in the early 1960s. Sometimes he'll bring a car to the Oakland show, or he may show up just to check things out and see some of the people in the business. He has also introduced other musicians to the rod & custom scene at the Oakland show. During the last few years, one of them was Eric Clapton, who now has his first custom-built street rod.

Vaughan has always been into cars. Born in Dallas, Texas, in 1951 he got into cars pretty early. "I learned about all kinds of car models through my uncle," he recalls, "because he was always pointing and asking me, 'What kind of car is that?'" Vaughan was 9 or 10 at the time, and he grew up reading the hot rod magazines like *Rod & Custom, Hop Up*, and *Car Craft*. "Like most kids, I was reading and checking out the custom cars in the books, and that started as soon as I could read," says Vaughan. Going to the store gave him a chance to page through the latest car

Mike Young's '60 Chevy (with Jimmie Vaughan's '51 Chevy in the background) was built by Gary Howard and designed by Vaughan. Howard started by chopping the top 3 inches before he cleaned all emblems and handles from the body. The front end was modified with '63 Olds headlights, a '59 Chevy bumper, and a custom grille. The abalone pearl-painted Chevy won the Barris d'Elegance Award at Oakland. *Steve Coonan*

It is easy to see that Jimmie Vaughan is very happy when his schedule makes it possible for him to visit places like Paso Robles and check out all the new custom cars. In 1999 he brought his Caddy and parked it outside the Paso Robles Inn, even if he had to take off and play two nights of the weekend in a nearby city.

magazines on the newsstand. He knew most of the George Barris, Larry Watson, and Ed "Big Daddy" Roth cars of the time.

The next natural step was to build model cars, and Vaughan got into them too. "In those days it was nearly considered destroying a car when modifications were done to them," explains Vaughan, "so I guess I felt like a little bit of a rebel liking all the Watson-style semi-customs." In the area where the family lived in Dallas, there were a few drive-in places nearby that Vaughan visited on his bicycle. To see some cars that were nosed, decked, and lowered was exciting to him.

It took him many years before he really got into building his own first custom car. Being a guy that likes the late 1950s and early 1960s style, Vaughan's cars are a re-creation of how the customs were done in those days. He is trying to recapture the custom cars he saw as a kid at the drive-in 40 years ago. Vaughan fits the picture just perfectly, too. He says that it should be called "restyling," because the GM cars of the early 1960s had great lines to begin with, and just need to be personalized to be great. Wild Watson-style paint jobs is something that he likes, too, but his own cars, so far, have been given one-color candy/pearl paint jobs.

Pictured here is Vaughan with his Fender Stratocaster and his latest Caddy custom in a studio photo session. He is not only a very good musician, but also has a good eye for creating very tasteful customs. No wonder he looks pleased, with his masterpiece in the background. *Steve Coonan*

Many years ago, Vaughan teamed up with custom builder (or restyler) Gary Howard in Georgetown, Texas. Together they have created some very nice, stunning customs. The first one they came up with was a '51 Chevy that Vaughan designed and Howard worked on. The Fleetline '51 was a Watson-style mild custom that was restyled twice before Howard painted it in "Violet Vision." The corners of the trunk, hood, and doors were rounded, and a set of '56 Chevy wheelwell lips were installed. Howard also restyled the front end with a new grille opening for a 31-tooth Corvette grille and frenched '54 Ford headlights. The rear was given the rounded look and a set of Rod Powell–made custom taillights. To make the Chevy ride nicely, a Nova front clip was added to the Fleetline, and in the rear the frame was C'd for more suspension travel. Lowering-blocks and airshocks made it work well. A tuck and roll interior in white and purple was made by Bruce of San Marcos. Vaughan has driven his Chevy to many events—even as far as the KKOA Nationals in Holland, Michigan, a couple of times.

The next custom the team built was a '63 Buick Riviera, which they finished in 1992. After the first look at the Riviera, you would think that it is just a cleaned-up Riv with a pretty paint job in a special lime gold candy. But Vaughan and Howard put a lot more into it than you might see at first. The top was chopped 2 inches, which gives the car a lower and nicer roofline, but is very hard for most people to see. Howard also extended the front fenders 1 inch around the large

Vaughan's '51 Chevy Fleetline was the first custom that he completed together with Gary Howard, and that was in the early 1990s. The look he wanted was an early Larry Watson–style mild custom. The chassis was updated with a Nova front clip and dropped with air shocks. The body had all the corners rounded and the wheel well lips from a '56 Chevy installed. Howard painted it in "violet vision" pearl.

This '63 Riviera was built in 1992 and was chopped 2 inches by Howard, to make the lines just perfect. Further, the suspension was lowered with cut springs, and the A-arms were dropped. The front fenders were extended 1 inch around the parking lights, and the hood had the peak taken out of it. Gary finished the car in a lime green candy paint. In the background we can see Vaughan's '51 Chevy, which was built before the Riviera. *Steve Coonan*

parking lights, and took the peak off the hood. To make it ride nice and low, the A-arms were dropped and the springs cut. It rolls on a set of '54 Buick Skylark wire wheels with whitewall tires. Vaughan also talked upholstery veteran Vernon McKean into doing a perfect '60s-style sculptured 1-inch roll and pleat in pearl white. Just like the show-winning custom interiors that McKean did in the early days, the Riviera interior is a piece of art. McKean is now like one of Vaughan's team. Vaughan won the Harry Bradley Design Achievement Award with the Riviera at the KKOA Nats in 1992.

Vaughan has also helped some of his friends build customs. The most published has been Mike Young's '60 Chevy Impala. Young and Vaughan are very close friends, so when Young was going to sell his stock '60 Chevy, Vaughan talked him into letting Howard "restyle" it instead. Vaughan went as far as telling Young, "If you don't like the Chevy when it is done, I'll trade you my Riviera for it." Young knew that Vaughan was serious about it, too. Vaughan put a lot of time into designing the Chevy, just as if it was his own new project. Vaughan gave the car a little wilder restyling than he usually gives his own cars, but it was still within the limits of improving the original lines it was given by the GM designers. Howard started with chopping the top 3 inches, which is still so subtle that people are not sure it is chopped at all. As with Vaughan's customs, Howard cleaned off all emblems and handles and rounded off all possible corners. He removed the

This night shot from Austin, Texas, shows three of the Jimmie Vaughan–designed cars, with his own '51 Chevy Fleetline and '63 Buick Riviera in the background behind Mike Young's '60 Chevy. *Steve Coonan*

To get some additional power under the hood, Vaughan ordered a stroked 526 long-block motor from C.M.D in Lakeland, Florida. It has a stroker crank, 9.2:1 compression, and a Cad Co hydraulic cam. On top of the motor there is a Latham blower with two handmade intake manifolds for the DCOE Weber carburetors.

INSET, LEFT: The rear wings of the '61 Caddy flow very well with the total design of the car, thanks to the 2-inch top chop by Howard. He also extended the trunk all the way down to the rear bumper.

Vaughan's latest is a '61 Caddy Coupe DeVille that was first presented at the Oakland show in 1999. Gary chopped it 2 inches and added the rear part of the roof from a four-door model. With airbags all around, Vaughan can cruise his custom as low as he wants to.

Howard's modifications to the front end bodywork are so subtle that many people will not even see it. He "pancaked" the hood and cut it down, and installed new hinges in the front instead. Howard filled the seams around the front fenders and also rounded the corners on the doors.

body lines on the quarter panels and front fenders and rounded off the rear fins. Both the front and rear were restyled. In the rear, Vaughan designed it to incorporate a pair of sunken handmade taillights by Jack Leick. The front end got a pair of '63 Olds headlights and a '59 Chevy bumper. Howard finished off the Chevy with a fabulous abalone metalflake/pearl lacquer paint job, which Rod Powell completed with some scallops and flames. Vernon McKean was again called upon to do the pearl white super tuck and roll interior. The Chevy was a success at the Oakland show, and Young, Vaughan, and the team ended up winning the prestigious George Barris Custom D'Eleganze Award. Winning the big awards means as much to Vaughan as winning a Grammy for his music, so Young gave the award to Vaughan. However, to get it right, Vaughan arranged to have the trophy duplicated, then gave the original to Young. Do you think Young wanted to trade the Chevy for Vaughan's Riv? No, he was very pleased with letting Vaughan and the boys "restyle" his old Chevy.

The latest in the line of Vaughan's customs is the '61 Caddy, which was finished just in time for the 50th Oakland show in 1999. To Vaughan, there is something very sexy and feminine in the lines of an early '60s Cadillac. The project got started when Vaughan shipped his Caddy to his friend Lee Pratt in Los Angeles to have the motor rebuilt and to do a quick semi-custom of it. Problems with getting the engine rebuilt soon turned up, so a new plan had to be made. With the car back in Austin, Texas, Vaughan's new plan was to do a bit more work on the Caddy, plus get another motor for it.

Howard and Vaughan took a closer look at the lines of the Cad before the work started. They just wanted to improve the lines and the total look. A 2-inch chop was the first thing that was done to get the smooth look. Howard used the rear part of the roof and the rear window from a four-door '61 Caddy to get more of a "flat-top" look. The body received a clean-up job, door corners

It is easy to see in this picture that Gary used a set of different hinges to reverse the opening of the hood. With the air-ride, Vaughan can drop the car down for the shows, but still raise it for freeway driving.

Vaughan likes the '54 Buick wire wheels, and they fit his Caddy well, with whitewall B.F.Goodrich Silvertown tires that give the car even more class.

were rounded off, and the hood was "pancaked." Howard also reversed the hood opening after the fenders were molded to the body. There was something different with this custom, compared to most other customs that are being built; Vaughan wanted some extra horsepower under the hood. It started when Vaughan got the information that a later 500-ci Caddy engine would be dropped into the '61. It was not really true, but after all was said and done, a stroked-'74 now-526-ci long-block was built for the car by CMD in Florida. The fully built motor received a Latham blower and two DCOE Weber carburetors on new manifolds. Roach in Austin (his real name is unknown) did the detailing and installation of the engine, after a special oil pan and a set of headers were made. The engine was dropped in the car with a beefed- up T.H. 400 transmission.

With this combination, Vaughan had a smooth, good-looking custom with plenty of extra power under the hood. The final touch was

The 1961 Caddy Coupe DeVille was just finished in time for the 50th Grand National Roadster Show. Vaughan, Howard, and all the others that helped out during the last few hectic weeks to finish the car did a good job. For many it was a very important show to be part of, and Jimmie Vaughan was one of them.

the paint job by Howard, in a special mix of House of Kolor green candy/pearl acrylic lacquer. The interior was done in black leather by Craig Willits of Rockwell, Texas. The Cad is rolling on a set of '54 Buick Skylark wire wheels, with B.F.Goodrich Silvertown whitewall tires. Vaughan even had the rear tires recapped to be slicks. To give the Caddy a low and smooth ride, the chassis was modified with Air-ride suspension, which gave him 4–5 inches that the car can be raised or lowered. Vaughan and Howard took their time finishing the Caddy, but with some extra people like Lee Pratt, Roach, and Craig Willits to help them out during the final assembly, they made it to the Oakland show in time. Since then, the Caddy has been published in many of the rod and custom magazines, and Jimmie Vaughan is definitely one of today's great creators and "restylers."

With the front fenders molded to the body, the hood was "pancaked" plus reversed, and a new line was created by Gary Howard to meet the grille. The stock headlights were replaced by two pairs of Lucas-type headlights, which used to be a very popular item among custom builders.

Richard Zocchi

This book would not be a complete picture of customizers and restylers on the West Coast without Richard Zocchi and his customs. Zocchi has been building his smooth-looking customs since the late 1950s. He lives in Walnut Creek in northern California, which is right in the middle of "custom country," with all the good metal masters and super painters around him in the Bay Area. Through the years, he has been winning most of the big awards and trophies that can be won with a custom. Zocchi and John D'Agostino have been competing at the big shows for more than 25 years with their latest creations. Most of the time they even have their displays next to each other at the shows. Even though they have always been competing, they have become good friends.

What got Zocchi started was a '53 Ford that he drove to high school and modified with a '54 Chevy grille, '56 Olds taillights, and Olds spinner caps. Zocchi dropped it down by reversing the spindles and C-ing the frame in the rear. After receiving a lot of good words about the Ford from his friends, he was hooked on customs and soon started to plan the next one. Before the 1961

The first custom that Richard Zocchi built was this '53 Ford, when he was still in high school in 1958. It was a mild custom that was nosed and decked, had a Chevy grille installed, and was painted in the hot '57 Chevy Sierra Gold metallic. At the time, he had no idea that he had a lifetime of building award-winning customs ahead of him. *Richard Zocchi*

Before the 1961 show season started, Zocchi had this '57 Olds hardtop customized. The emblems and door handles were removed from the body. A '58 Buick grille and chromed reversed wheels were added and the suspension lowered, before Gene Winfield painted it in a gold candy. *Richard Zocchi*

Maybe the first real "Zocchi-look" car was this '62 Pontiac Grand Prix, which was brand new when he drove it to Winfield's shop to get it modified. All the chrome trim, emblems, and door handles were shaved off the body, headlights were frenched, plus the rear fenders extended a few inches before it was painted in Winfield's first metalflake job. This picture shows it later in the 1962 season, after it was repainted in a tangerine candy. *Gene Winfield*

This '64 Buick Wildcat was also a brand-new car when Zocchi started out with it. Bill Hines installed hydraulics on it, and it might just have been the first-ever West Coast custom with that feature installed. Another first was the Winfield paint job in green-blended candy with Murano pearl on top, which made it flip-flop in different colors. *Richard Zocchi*

show season got started, Zocchi had his first Winfield-built car. It was a '57 Olds hardtop, which received a cleaned-up body, a '58 Buick grille, and a lowered suspension. With a gold candy Winfield paint job, it was easy to see "the clean Zocchi look" that later was going to be very familiar in the custom world.

The Olds was a big hit at the shows, and Zocchi was on a roll, planning another new car right away. At the time, some of the customizers were buying brand-new cars and taking them to pros like Gene Winfield to have them modified and restyled and get a fabulous candy or pearl paint job. But they all had something in common: they needed to be lowered. "Yeah, you have to drop all customs to make them sit and look right," says Zocchi.

The first brand-new car that Zocchi customized was a '62 Pontiac Grand Prix, which he

drove to Winfield's shop directly from the Pontiac dealer. When he first showed it at the 1962 Oakland Show, it had only 200 miles on the speedometer. With the Pontiac, the Zocchi look was perfected. After that he worked together with Winfield on just improving the lines of the great-looking Grand Prix. When the headlights were frenched, rear fenders extended a few inches, and the grille reworked with bullets, Winfield performed one of his first metalflake paint jobs in lime green. The car won the very prestigious Custom D'Eleganze Award at the Oakland show, and Richard Zocchi's name was now for the first time in both the history books and the magazines. "Winfield did all the modifications and paint for $750," notes Zocchi, "which was his cost and about half what it should have been. Later during that same year, all the clear on top of the metalflake started to crack up, so I had Winfield repaint

One of Richard Zocchi's all-time custom favorites is Joe Bailon's '57 Buick, *Candy Wagon*, so in 1977 he built his own version of it. The top was chopped 3 inches by Rod Powell, the body rechromed, and the headlights frenched before Himsl/Haas painted it in red candy. *Richard Zocchi*

the car in a tangerine candy." With the new candy paint, the Pontiac won big awards both at the San Mateo Show and the Oakland show in early 1963, before Bob Tingle (who built the famous Orange Crate show '32 Ford sedan) walked in at the Oakland show and bought the car.

Zocchi's next project was a brand-new '64 Buick Wildcat, which was lowered by Bill Hines. It also had hydraulics installed, which just might have been the first West Coast custom with that type of suspension. "People were shocked when they saw me nearly drop that thing on the ground," says Zocchi. It received all of its bodywork and paint at Winfield's shop. The Wildcat had the first Winfield candy paint job in combination with some Murano pearl on top of it, which changed colors in different lights. The Wildcat was also a big show winner.

During the next 10 years Zocchi built additional more cars, but most of them were for use on the street and were not show cars. In 1974, however, he was back on track after he saw a '50 Mercury in the back of Dick Falk's shop in nearby Concord, California. After he had talked Falk into selling him the Merc, he got started on it with Bill Reasoner and Art Himsl. The chopped and perfect Merc was called *Cool 50*, and it had a 302 Ford small-block under the hood. "The *Cool 50* blew everybody away," says Zocchi, "especially with the red candy paint and the super- nice white Ken Foster interior." It was first shown in 1976 and it won many big awards during the following years, including the Sam Barris Memorial Award. After being published in many magazines and on the cover of *Custom Rodder* in 1980, the car was sold to Show Promotions, which has been touring it ever since.

The next big winner was a '57 Buick that was built by Himsl and Haas in Salinas. Zocchi notes, "I liked Joe Bailon's *Candy Wagon* Buick so much that I wanted my own version of it, I guess." Rod Powell chopped the Buick three inches before the body was de-chromed and the headlights were frenched. Art Himsl painted the dropped Buick in red candy.

Zocchi's next car was also a borrowed idea, but this time from Joe Wilhem, who had built a famous '58 Chrysler New Yorker in black in 1959.

This '54 Mercury was built at Bill Reasoner's shop in 1981. The chop-top Merc included a Carson top, a '52 DeSoto grille, and '56 Packard taillights; it was painted dark blue metallic. *Richard Zocchi*

Zocchi built another classic custom in 1985—this '41 Ford Coupe. Paul Blatt did the top chopping, and much of the other work—including the paint—was done at Bill Reasoner's shop. Art Himsl finished the white pearl Reasoner paint with some pink pearl flames. *Richard Zocchi*

Richard and Cherie Zocchi's garage at their home in Walnut Creek, California, is very impressive, with four of their award-winning customs parked on a red carpet. The latest winner is the purple '56 Dodge, which was finished in time for the 2000 Oakland show.

One of the walls in Zocchi's garage features a large painting depicting most of his cars through the years. Zocchi had the artist come back now and then to add some new cars to the painting, so you can wonder if he is going to run out of space.

The '39 Dodge Coupe was an odd car to start with, but Zocchi saw the potential to make a great custom out of it. It was built in 1992, and Armando Hernandez did all the bodywork, including chopping the top and creating a new front end with dual Lincoln headlights. Bill Reasoner and Art Himsl did the soft pearl paint job.

This '63 Olds Starfire was just finished for the 1998 Oakland show, and the bodywork was performed by Logan Davis. Darryl Hollenbeck at Acme Customs in Antioch, California, did the light pastel purple pearl paint. The car next to the Olds is the '57 Buick that was built in 1990 with the top chopped by Rod Powell and painted by Reasoner/Himsl.

Zocchi found a good '58 Chrysler for sale, and for modifications he once again took it to Gene Winfield, who had just opened his shop in Canoga Park, California, and the car was named *Golden Sunrise* after the blended candy paint in gold/tangerine and white pearl. Before it was painted, the top was chopped a few inches, the body re-chromed, and the fins extended—a perfect combination of the Zocchi look and a Winfield paint job. The car won awards at all the shows in 1980.

In 1981 it was time for something different for Zocchi, and that was going to be a '54 Mercury with a Carson top, built at Bill Reasoner's shop. The Merc was given '56 Packard taillights, Olds headlights, and a DeSoto grille. Ken Foster did another super-nice interior job, and the car was painted dark blue metallic. Then came another Merc, this time a chopped '51 that Frank DeRosa and Rod Powell collaborated on. It had a DeSoto grille and a set of '54 Mercury taillights. Zocchi first showed it in 1983 before he sold it to his friend, Bill Reasoner. In 1984 he was planning for an early 1940s car, so he built a '41 Ford that was chopped and had a '47 Old's grille. It was painted

A '56 Chrysler Windsor is not a common model for custom building, but Zocchi wanted to do something extra with it. He took it to John Aiello at Acme in Antioch, California, who chopped it and gave it the Zocchi styling, before Himsl mixed the baby blue pearl paint for it. Most Zocchi customs are full-sized, and the 1956 Chrysler is a good example of that.

in white pearl by Reasoner and had flames done by Himsl. In 1990, Zocchi was building another '57 Buick. This time it was chopped by Butch Hurley and was painted in pearl by Reasoner, with scallops by Himsl. Zocchi still has this Buick and showed it a few years ago at the Oakland show again. In 1990 it won the Sam Barris Memorial Award, and was given a set of '56 Old's headlights, Packard taillights, and a 3-inch chopped top. "I always liked the pastel colors and Reasoner," Zocchi remembers, "and Himsl got me the right soft shades of pearl."

In 1991 Zocchi was inducted into the Hall of Fame at the Oakland show, and he already was planning for the next great winner: a '39 Dodge full custom coupe. The Dodge is an odd car to begin with, but Zocchi had Armando Hernandez in Antioch, California, do a lot of body modifications to give it a very impressive look. Hernandez chopped the top and totally changed the front end with dual '58 Lincoln headlights and a '39 LaSalle grille. Again, Reasoner and Himsl painted, this time in a near-pink and cream pearl. The Dodge won the George Barris D'Eleganze Award

The year was 1997 when Richard Zocchi debuted this '55 Lincoln Coupe at the Oakland Show, and then later took it to the Paso Robles event for the Friday-night cruising. The car did very well at the shows with many big wins. John Aiello did the bodywork and Darryl Hollenbeck painted it.

at the Oakland show, plus Best of Show at Paso Robles the same year. The Dodge coupe is still parked in Zocchi's garage.

In 1993 it was time for another Dodge, this time a '57 with big fins. The work was done at John Aiello's shop in Antioch, California. It was chopped and the rocker panels were extended, to give the car the illusion of being lower than it was. Zocchi called on Winfield to paint it in a blended gold and cream pearl color. This car also won its share of awards; the biggest was the Joe Bailon Most Beautiful Custom Award at the

Sacramento Show. The Dodge was soon sold, and his eyes were now looking for another early Olds for his next project.

A '51 Olds was the car he decided on after looking at some other early '50s Oldsmobiles. John Aiello did the chopping and the rest of the bodywork before Himsl painted it in a pastel yellow and cream pearl to make another perfect Zocchi look. The modifications included '56 Olds headlights and a '54 Corvette grille. Again, he won the George Barris D'Eleganze Award at the Oakland show, plus Best of Show at the Paso

For the 1999 season Zocchi built a new Lincoln, this time a full-size '56 Premier. It was chopped, and John Aiello at the Acme shop put in many weeks of bodywork. Finally, Darryl Hollenbeck painted it. Air-Ride has been installed on most of Zocchi's cars during the last several years. The frenched '56 Olds headlights and the tight grille are some of Zocchi's trademarks. The front bumper is from a '58 Caddy.

John Aiello chopped the top of the big Lincoln 5 inches, which makes the car look even longer and lower. The rear fenders were modified with a set of '54 Packard taillights. On top of the cream white and yellow paint, Hollenbeck used some extra gold pearl.

The new custom for 2000 is this '56 Dodge, which again was built at the Acme Custom Shop, with the bodywork done by John Aiello. The chopped top and a totally redone front end with a new grille and a set of frenched '56 Olds headlights is Zocchi style. Under the hood you will find a small Red Ram hemi.

Robles event the same year, in 1994. In 1995 his choice for a new project was an odd '56 Chrysler that not many people ever customized. Once again he took it to John Aiello in Antioch and had it chopped, and when the rest of the Zocchi-look modifications were done to the body, Himsl came up with new baby blue pastel colors for it. It was another big winner that won

its class at Oakland and Sacramento before winning the Goodguys Custom Rod D'Eleganze Award in 1996.

Zocchi has built many very nice customs, but one of his best is without a doubt the '55 Lincoln with the right-on name *The Mark of Zocchi*, which was finished for the 1996 shows. John Aiello chopped it and made plenty of small

The smooth lines and extended rear fenders make it harder to identify this car. Rounded corners on the doors, trunk, and hood is an old customizer's trick that gives a custom plenty of additional class. The purple and white pearl was applied by Marcos Garcia.

Richard Zocchi wants his details as fine as he can get them, so all the pieces in the dash were re-chromed before the new interior was finished in matching white and two shades of purple. A console was made between the seats and the chromed letter "Z" says it all.

modifications to make all the proportions just right, and Darryl Hollenbeck painted it in a pastel yellow pearl. For the 1998 season, a '63 Olds Starfire was given the Zocchi treatment by Logan Davis and then painted by Darryl Hollenbeck.

Zocchi's two latest projects are a 1956 Lincoln Premier and a 1956 Dodge in lavender pearl paint; he unveiled the Dodge at the 2000 Oakland show. Both cars were modified at Aiello's shop in Antioch; Darryl Hollenbeck painted the Lincoln, while Marcos Garcia painted the Dodge.

Whatever car Zocchi picks for his projects, they will always be finished with long smooth lines, impressive chrome, and fantastic pastel paint jobs with matching interiors. A Richard Zocchi custom can always be spotted right away in a show, not just by the pastel paint, but also by the super finish.

Customs in Primer

In the early days of customs, during the late 1940s and early 1950s, primer was an important step in getting a car painted. After modifications—such as a nose and deck job, filling door handle holes, or chopping—were completed, the primer was sprayed on to prevent the bare metal from rusting. Many times, the bodywork was done over a long period of time, piece by piece, so the primer came in handy. During the last 20 to 25 years it has become more of an "in" thing to leave a custom in a primer, or "suede," paint job. It not only makes for a cool nostalgia look, but the owner doesn't need to feel pressured that the car has to be perfect. This also means it can be driven daily, because the finish is not as sensitive as an expensive candy or pearl paint job. Most custom owners and builders who spray their cars with primer today have already decided that that's it: no paint; just primer. It is not just for cars "under construction" anymore. For years now, the special "hot rod primer" has been available in spray cans, which is perfect to use for smaller parts and panels.

The younger generation of custom owners and builders are more into the primer look than others,

Skip Newton from Las Vegas built this '57 Ford Ranchero with plenty of old custom tricks. He tunneled the headlights and taillights and cleaned the body of all chrome trim before he painted it in a lilac, with a lot of flattener to get the primer look. Skip cut the frame so he could lower it with air shocks. Under the hood you will find a 292-inch Y-block motor.

This East Coast '50 Mercury is owned by Thomas Midolo, and it has been chopped more than we have ever seen before. Talk about "mail-slot"windows! The hubcaps are Caddy "Sombreros" that go well with the wide whitewalls. The flames give the black primer paint job further style.

so it is their older-style customs you see in primer. They like '50 Mercurys, '54 Chevys, and '50 Fords, just to name a few types. More and more young guys are getting into customs. Their earlier interests and activities might have been skateboarding, graffiti-painting, and punk music, but they are now getting into customs through swing, blues, and rockabilly music and other retro trends. You're being a bit of a rebel if you drive a custom in black primer. That is the common thing among the new generation of custom owners and builders.

After years of using regular lacquer primers in their favorite colors (black, gray, and oxide red), smart young custom builders like Cole Foster in Salinas, California, started to mix their own

"primers." Instead of real primer, Foster began to use regular paint with flattener to get a primer that would not wear down as quickly. After that, he tried regular metallics with flattener, adding some pearl white to the mix to get extra highlights over the round corners and fenders. With that idea, you can use nearly any color and make it semi-gloss for a primer look, but still get some shine. Today some paint suppliers even have semi-gloss clear—a good thing to use over new primer if the car owner wants to keep it in perfect shape for years to come.

Foster more or less started a new trend in "primers" in northern California during the last few years, and it may very well spread. The best

Many of today's rock 'n' roll stars also have a passion for custom cars. Mike Ness (Social Distortion) is cleaning his chopped and custom-built '54 Chevy. The semi-gloss-black-painted Chevy was chopped by Cole Foster in Salinas, California.

Cole Foster from Salinas, California, is one of the young customizers who got the trend going by using metallics and flattener to make the modern-style primers. His "shop-truck" is a good example of this type of paint. The truck is a '53 Chevy pickup with a 4-inch chop, which Cole painted in Red Rose metallic with some white pearl and a lot of flattener.

The Choppers, a car club in Burbank, California, have a bunch of old-style customs, and this 6-inch-chopped '41 Ford is owned by Deron Wright. It also has frenched headlights and full fender skirts. On top of that good bodywork is a gold metallic paint job with flattener.

Today you can see all kinds of colors with the primer look, especially at events like West Coast Customs in Paso Robles. The green chopped '52 Dodge in the foreground and the chopped '54 Chevy in copper metallic, which belongs to Jesus Villabos, both were sprayed with flattener for a primer look.

known of Foster's customs is his shop truck, a '54 Chevy pickup that was chopped and had its body cleaned up before he painted it in a dark rose-red metallic with plenty of flattener, plus some white pearl added in the mix. That paint job made a big impact on young customizers all over the West Coast, especially after it was featured in some of the rod and custom car magazines.

When it comes to the real primers, you will find all kinds of specialized products at the paint suppliers for aluminum, fiberglass, steel, and so on. You use the primers to fill with, before you do the final sanding and apply the topcoats, but most builders use it to get the "suede look." It is a good idea to stay with the same brand of paint

through all of the components that you use; this way there is less chance of having problems such as poor adhesion, crazing, and fogging. Today's low-pressure, high-volume spray guns make it easier to apply the primers and create less over-spray. New types of primers and spray guns have been introduced to keep the painters healthier, but painters still should protect themselves with a high-quality respirator and special clothing.

Today's primers are a little more complicated than earlier ones. These days there are etching primers, which are applied in thin coats before applying a topcoat of sanding primer, less than 24 hours after the first coat dries. The etching primer will oxidate if a topcoat is not applied.

Bill Ross built this '46 Ford custom with a Lincoln Zephyr front end and '50 Buick rear fenders. He drove his custom in primer to the 1998 Paso Robles event. Later, he painted it in a bright green candy and won numerous awards at the 50th Oakland Roadster Show.

After the top (sanding) primer is sanded, a sealer is used. One more good thing with the new types of primers is that they will dry to a semi-gloss finish and give a real "suede look." The color of the primer you see more than anything else is Krylon semi-gloss black, which is a primer favorite for many custom builders. Several are even referring to that spray can primer as the color they want their cars to be painted.

Many of today's big names in customizing bring their new cars to Paso Robles in primer, then finish the cars during the fall so they can bring them to the Oakland show in January. If you like customs in primer, Paso is the place to

Eric Hulsers's chopped '54 Plymouth has a black primer as a base with scallops and flames as an extra decoration. In a case like this, where there are plenty of hours and money involved in the paint job, it is a good idea to protect it with the new semi-gloss clear.

Cole Foster built this '60 Ford *Starliner* semi-custom a few years ago, and he painted it in a light green metallic with plenty of flattener and extra white pearl in the mix. With this paint he also tried the new semi-gloss clear paint, to make the paint last longer. The *Starliner* was later sold to one of the boys in the Choppers.

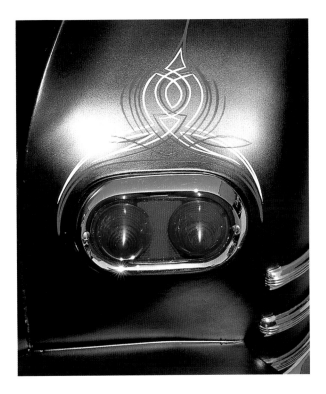

Black primer and pin-striping go well together, as, for example, around this '50 Buick taillight on a custom. Pinstriping is coming back more and more. At most bigger rod and custom events, you can see pin-stripers in action with their brushes and one-shot paint.

Plenty of rock stars are into custom cars, and this chopped '50 Mercury is owned by Brett Read, the drummer in the band Rancid. The clean body was painted with Krylon black primer, to get it just right. Brett also owns a fenderless '32 roadster in black primer, with whitewall tires and a small-block plus four-speed under the hood.

The designer and pin-striper Steve Stanford is well known for his illustrations of 1950s and 1960s full-size modified cars. When he chose a car for personal transportation, it had to have great lines. His choice was a two-door '58 Chevy that was given some simple modifications, like lowering, whitewall tires on steel wheels with Caddy caps and a tube grille. The paint is light blue with plenty of flattener for a primer look, and some white scallops to give the paint job additional class.

The sun is doing a lot to give the flat metallic paint jobs the best luster. In this case, it is a '50 Chevy with frenched headlights and custom grille that was given a dark silver paint job with white scallops. In the background, there is a '50 Mercury custom in flat copper metallic.

see them during Memorial Day Weekend. One of the best-known cars in primer was Bill Ross' '46 Ford, which he drove from Yakima, Washington, to Paso Robles to be part of the show in 1998. Later the same year, the car was painted in a bright green candy and entered in the Oakland show, where it won the Barris D'Eleganze award.

Another famous car that was run in purple and gray primer for some time was Jimmie Vaughan's '51 Chevy. Gary Howard in Austin, Texas built the car, and Vaughan drove it to many events around the country before he decided

to let Howard paint it in a lavender pearl. Vaughan took the car to both Paso Robles and the Oakland Roadster Show in the early 1990s.

A great early-style custom in flat paint is Deron Wright's radically chopped '41 Ford Coupe in a metallic gold. Wright, who is a member of The Choppers Club, has recently redone his coupe with a '47 Olds grille and a dark green metallic flat paint job. Wright and his friends in The Choppers are good examples of today's new generation of primer-custom builders of whom we now see more and more.

Naked Beauty

I ran into Terry Hageman about 15 or 16 years ago when he moved out to the West Coast to start working for Boyd Coddington. It was during this period that he worked together with the Swedes, Jarmo Pulkkinen and Ingemar Becker. I have a feeling that all three will continue to remember very well what happened during these years, because they had fun working together, which resulted in a lot of impressive work. Terry did some metalwork and prepared the cars for paint. He had a lot of knowledge about metalwork and it wasn't long before he started to think about opening his own shop. Some time later, he rented a shop in Fountain Valley and got started on his own. A lot of his current work is not just hot rods or customs, but bodies for Sprint Cars and Midgets. He has many friends and customers running these racecars, so it is natural that he will do their metal work as well.

In his spare time, Terry owns enough cars to usually have something fun to drive. Earlier, it was a wine-red '32 Roadster, but now he is driving a tuned, flathead-powered '39 Ford Coupe. He is also working on a '51 Mercury that has been chopped 3 inches in the front and 4 inches in the rear. He also frenched the headlights, rounded corners on the hood, and modified the rear fenders with '54 Mercury taillights. They say that you need to make 140 cuts in the top to make a good top chop on a '49–'51 Mercury, and that can be found on Terry's Mercury. The rear window is from a '50 Mercury. The car is built in traditional custom style and under the hood there is an Olds Rocket motor, or that is what most people think. It is actually a brand-new 350 Chevy crate motor, which has been dressed up like an Olds with old valvecovers and an early manifold for the right look. Behind the motor is a late manual Camaro transmission. The chassis was updated with a 9-inch Ford rear end from a '63 Ford pickup and the front end has dropped spindles. The "naked," clean steel body looks like a piece of art in his workshop, and it is not often that you can see a perfect custom like this before it gets a few layers of primer. It is nearly a pity to have it painted, because people should see all the good metalwork that Terry did.

Pictured here are Terry Hageman and his piece of art, the '51 Mercury that has been his hobby and weekend work for the last few years. The top has been chopped 3 inches in front and 4 inches in the rear, but he was not 100 percent pleased with it the first time, so he did it again. The softspoken and hardworking Hageman has done a lot of nice cars through the years for his customers, but his own new Mercury will get him more ink in the magazines than ever before.

The difference between the '50 and '51 Mercury is the longer rear fenders on the '51. Hageman extended and modified the fenders for a set of '54 Mercury taillights, the trunk has been given rounded corners, and the perfectly chopped top now has a '50 rear window. The rear bumper is the stock '51 Merc, but Hageman shortened it to tuck in closer to the body.

The front end has been massaged to perfection by Hageman, which included frenching a set of '52 Ford headlights, rounding the corners on the hood, and modifying the grille opening. The grille was made from a '54 Pontiac grille with bullets in brass by Hageman. The front bumper has been shortened 2 inches in each end and the guards have been shortened 5 inches.

Shows

More custom cars are being built today than in other years, which means that more and more cars are also being entered in shows. Since the day that Al Slonaker opened his Grand National Roadster show to hot rods and customs in 1950, it has been the main show for the custom builders. It's no wonder so many of the well-known custom builders have been based in northern California, where they have the big shows and events. Slonaker called Sam and George Barris in Los Angeles to ask that some of the southern California customs be included at the first show. The Barris brothers entered a custom Buick/Caddy Convertible in the 1950 Oakland Show, where many other customs were entered too.

One of the best-known customs at the Oakland show in the early days was Joe Bailon's *Miss Elegance*, a '41 Chevy that was entered in 1952. The car was not yet finished then, but Slonaker still wanted it in the show, just because it had a very spectacular dash, with a massive amount of gauges, buttons, and even a built-in bar. In 1953, Bailon brought the finished car back, with a 3-inch chop, filled quarter windows, extended rear

The most famous custom car of the early days was no doubt Bob Hirohata's Barris-built '51 Mercury, which was finished in 1952. Hirohata won 184 major trophies with it before he sold it in 1955. The top was chopped and made into a hardtop. Frenched headlights, extended hood lip, and a totally reworked grille opening and grille, were just some of the items modified by the Barris Brothers in 1952.

This '39 Mercury was also custom built in the early 1950s by Barris, who gave it the full treatment. It is in the same style as the other famous Barris '39 Mercs of Nick Matranga and Johnny Zaro. The chopped top got the same-type windows as the Zaro Merc, and the suspension was dropped with a C'd frame before the fender skirts were added. Most of the early Barris customs had a dark metallic paint job, like this wine red color on Ron Martinez's Merc.

fenders, and a handmade tube grille. He painted the custom Chevy in a deep maroon color. Since then, Bailon has built many show-winning customs and has won nine Custom D'Eleganze trophies for "Best Custom" at the Oakland show. Even if most of us are not old enough to have been part of the custom scene at the first real rod and custom show at the Oakland Exposition Building in January 1950, it was much of a repeat at the 50th show in 1999. At this special anniversary of the "Granddaddy" of all shows, promotor Don Tognotti did everything he could do to get as many old winners as possible to attend.

When it comes to customs, the all-time favorite of many fans is still Bob Hirohata's Barris-built '51 Mercury. Even if Hirohata never took the car to the Oakland show, he drove it to the L.A. Motorama in 1952, right after the car was finished, and it won some big trophies. Hirohata sold the car in 1955 after winning 184 major trophies at shows from L.A. to Indy. Since 1959, the car has been in the hands of Jim McNeil in Orange,

California, who found it for sale at a used car lot for $500. For many years, McNeil has been in the process of restoring the old custom. For the special "The Men & Machines" exhibition at the Oakland Museum in 1997, the car was shown again, although the interior was not finished at the time. Two years later, McNeil brought the Hirohata Merc to the Oakland show for the first time, where it was just on display and not included in the competition for the trophies this time. Hundreds of Mercurys have been built worldwide, and many custom builders through the years looked at the Hirohata car as the perfect custom. Winning all the trophies at the shows in the early years gave the Hirohata Merc much ink in the magazines.

The West Coast has hosted many different shows in various cities through the years, but the Oakland show is still the granddaddy when it comes to customs. Another exhibition with big custom status is the Sacramento show, which today has the same owner and organizer as the

The '51 Olds is a popular model for all custom builders, and Rich Shavez took his to John Aiello for all the modifications. The top was chopped, front fenders extended, suspension lowered with air-ride, and Corvette teeth used for the grille. The paint is a typical northern California—style smooth yellow pearl with some white scallops.

Oakland show, Dan Cyr. Many of the big names have entered their cars at Oakland, and then kept the cars in the area in order to go to the Sacramento show some weeks later.

Of the outdoor shows and events, the West Coast Customs event at Paso Robles, California, during Memorial Day Weekend is the one that has cruising as well as a big show in the park, right in the middle of the city. All the big custom names in the business come to Paso Robles with their latest custom creations. The bonus for attendees is not only to see the cars in the show, but also to watch them cruise down the main street on Friday night. Big names like John D'Agostino, Richard Zocchi, Rick Dore, and Gene Winfield have shown off their latest creations at Paso Robles during the past 15 years. The long holiday weekend is perfect for cruising in Paso, and many of the nearly 1,000 cars that attend this event will start turning up on Thursday afternoon.

Friday night is cruising night on the main street, and people sit all along the street to see the

Frank Livingston is a well-known custom owner in the Bay Area, and this is his latest. The '49 Chevy fastback has been updated with a '79 Olds front clip in the chassis department, plus a 305 Chevy under the hood with a 350 T.H. transmission. The bodywork and paint were done by Dan Pimentel and Darryl Hollenbeck.

The *Golden Ruby*, a '50 Ford, is owned by Ted Thomas, all the way from North Carolina. It was built by Kory Petty in Tulsa, Oklahoma; it has been nosed and decked, the headlights and taillights are frenched, and the door corners rounded. It was painted by Kory Petty. The chassis was updated with a Mustang II–type front end, S10 rear end, and a Chevy 350/350 combination. At the Oakland show in 2000, the car won the Best Custom Paint award, and Steve Stella, who striped the car, won the Von Dutch award.

John D'Agostino presented two new Cadillacs at the 1998 Oakland show, and *Marilyn*, in gold pearl, is a '53 Eldorado that was restyled by John Aiello and Darryl Hollenbeck in D'Agostino's hometown, Antioch, California. The windshield was chopped 3-1/2 inches before the Carson-style top (not on the car in the picture) was made for it. The raspberry red *Cool '57* already had some custom work done by Gene Winfield when D'Agostino bought it and had Aiello and Hollenbeck do the rest of the work before Hollenbeck painted it.

fabulous customs come by. Dore, Zocchi, and all the other big names cruise their Oakland show winners that night. At the end of the street is an A&W burger drive-in that features live music during the cruise, and at the 1999 event the Hot Rod Trio from southern California gave us some great old rockabilly tunes.

Paso Robles is not the only event arranged by West Coast Customs; they also have one in October at the pier parking lot in Huntington Beach, California. This event draws more of the local cars, but during the past few years more and more cars make the drive from northern California, Arizona, and so on. This get-together is called "Back to the Beach" and is one of the events that most of the new-generation hot rod and custom clubs want to attend. Rows of old-style customs in black primer are what you can expect at this event.

Richard Zocchi has been building customs since the 1960s, and he is still creating some of the most stunning cars in the business today. He came to the 50th Oakland Show with this '56 Lincoln custom in white and yellow pearl, with his trademark chrome wire wheels and wide whitewalls.

The cruising in Paso Robles on the Friday-night West Coast Customs event is something very special, and people are sitting along the main street all the way. Some of the most fabulous customs in the country will be cruising by that night.

Paso Robles Inn, right in the middle of town, is where you can find most of the pro-built customs during the Memorial Day Weekend event. People are checking out all the cruising cars on the main street, and the cars parked outside the hotel.

The KKOS (Kustom Kemps of Sweden) had its first Nationals during 1999 at Strömsholms Castle in Hallstahammar, and it was a big step for the club to organize the event. Ola Thorslund is one of the guys in charge of this event, and this '55 Mercury, *Lady Lime*, in the foreground, is his. The pearl white, chopped '55 Ford in the background belongs to Micke Öhman. Among the modifications were changing it from a four-door to a two-door hardtop and extending the fenders.

Most of the new-generation clubs have members with both hot rods and customs, but all are old '40s- and '50s-style cars, so it is a mix, even if the customs dominate. We have also seen a new trend in '60s "semi-customs" in the last few years, and the Sultans from Long Beach are always at the Beach event with 20 to 25 cars. "Restyling," as Jimmie Vaughan calls it, is just a way of giving a good-looking '60s car a cleaner look, and with a lowering job and a set of whitewall tires on wire wheels, you have a Sultans-style semi-custom.

There are many other good custom shows and events around the country, like Kustom Kemps Of America's Nationals event in Holland, Michigan, which even some of the West Coast customizers attend. There's also KKOA's Lead Sled Spectacular in Kentucky. The big one on the East Coast is Terry Cook's Lead East, which most years has more than 1,700 cars in the parking lot at the Hilton in Parsippinay, New Jersey. This event takes place over Labor Day Weekend, and Cook is not kidding when he says that "it is

This '51 Mercury convertible, built by Gene Winfield, has a chopped Carson top, frenched headlights, and a very nice bronze candy paint job. It is now owned by Håkan Johansson in Bålsta, Sweden, who is a member the KKOS over there.

The parking lot at the pier in Huntington Beach is filled with customs when West Coast Kustoms holds its fall event there. You see more cars in black primer at this event than anywhere else, and the younger generation custom builders come out with all their friends in the clubs.

The '57 Buick is a model that many custom builders use because it is so perfect to begin with. This custom has a nose and deck job, cleaned-off emblems and handles, plus frenched headlights. Lowering, whitewall tires on a set of Buick wire wheels, a candy paint job, and a tuck and roll interior in pearl white is all you need for a neat custom like Terry Foster's, from Lodi, California.

Bo Sandberg was one of the pioneers in Sweden who created the first rod and custom shows, plus the *Colorod* magazine. Sandberg also built some of the most extreme cars, like this '59 Thunderbird that he called *Wild Bird*, which he built in the late 1960s. The top was cut, and an extra trunk, turned forward, was used to cover the back-seat space. The rear part of the top was used for the roll bar. Sandberg painted it in silver Metalflake with one blue and one red stripe on the driver's side.

the biggest 50s party anywhere." There have been many great-looking customs built on the East Coast through the years, and some of those are now restored and in the mix of cars at Lead East today.

The custom car scene is not just thriving in the United States, because in many countries throughout the world, customized cars are being built every day. In Europe there are clubs and events in nearly all countries, most notably England, Germany, Finland, Norway, and my old home country, Sweden. There is a Kustom Kemp of Sweden club that is a part of the KKOA, and they hold their own events every summer. In 1999, the club arranged its first Nationals at Strömsholms Castle in Hallstahammar. Maybe it doesn't sound like much when 50 customs attend the event, but the club was pretty happy with it. The Nationals are now growing again, and many more cars are expected to be entered in the future.

The metalflake paint jobs that were introduced on the market in the 1960s are now coming back on the custom scene. When people are recreating these style customs, it is natural that the style of paint comes with them. Don Shaver from Hemet, California, owns this chopped '54 Chevy hardtop that has modified taillights and frenched headlights and is painted in silver Glowble.

You can wonder why Ford didn't make this little neat coupe, instead of the Business Coupe. The design from Steve Stanford and the work by Pete Chapouris' team gave Billy Gibbons a very unique custom car. After that, the car was updated with a Fat-man front clip, a Mustang II front

end, a Ford 9-inch rear end, and the metalworkers spent about 500 hours on the top and door modifications. The doors are now 10 inches longer and the roof was chopped 3-1/2 inches before the rear part was made into the three-window style.

Billy G's '50 Ford "Kopperhed" Coupe

When ZZ Top's Billy Gibbons first took his 1950 Ford Business Coupe to Pete Chapouris (at the time, his shop was PC3G before it was renamed So Cal Speedshop), the plan was to give it a clean-up job and maybe some mild modifications. The plan changed radically, however, after he got some drawings from Steve Stanford. Stanford suggested some further modifications and also suggested making it into a three-window coupe, kind of like a 1950s concept car. Billy liked the idea very much, so he got Pete and his people working on it.

The first step was to get it lowered, as well as to give it better handling and brakes. A Fat-man Fabrication front clip with a Mustang II front suspension gave the car a 4-inch drop, enhanced handling, and improved brakes. The frame was cut by the firewall, and the new clip was welded on. The rear end was replaced by a new 9-inch Ford from Currie that was mounted with the stock springs de-arced, to drop the rear a few inches.

Most people think that this is a stock '50 Ford Coupe and they cannot say what is strange with the design of it. Maybe it is because the design, as Pete Chapouris said, "[is] the first radical custom that has not been nosed and decked or frenched." The emblems and doorhandles were left on the car to get the stock appearance to 100 percent. The 16-inch steel wheels with whitewall tires fit the car perfectly.

Billy Gibbons and the other boys in the Texas boogie band ZZ-Top were all in place when the '50 Ford *Kopperhed* was first modeled at the Petersen Museum in L.A. The car was Billy's, but the boys in the band were there for the first press showing of the new car. As always, Billy was very much involved in all the decisions made in the process of having the car built.

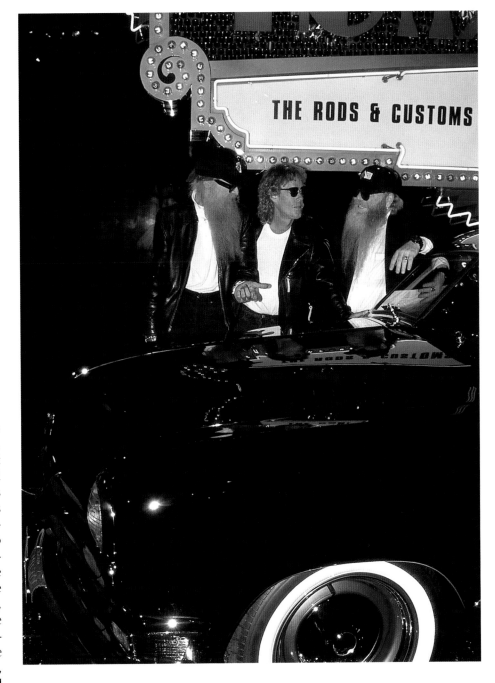

When it came to the engine for the car, Billy wanted a rebuilt 312-inch Y-block Ford with three carburetors just for the good looks of it. Most of the working hours were still to come in the body modifications. It took more than 500 hours for the metalworkers to cut, weld, and finish the door and roof alterations. First it had to be chopped 3-1/2 inches, and a 3/4-inch strip had to be added in the middle of the roof. The rear top part with the window leaned forward after it was slid down below the rear panel. To form the 10-inches-longer doors, six '50 Ford doorskins and four door openings were used to get all the pieces in place.

The result was a stock-looking '50 Ford in a three-window coupe look that most people would think came that way from Ford. To finish the whole project off, a white and copper tuck and roll interior was done by Ron Mangus. The name came from Billy, who thought the colors of the car and interior reminded him off the "Kopperhed" snake, from back home in Texas. The car made its exhibition debut at the Petersen Museum in L.A., but since then Billy has put a lot of miles on the odometer.

Custom Clubs

I got in touch with the Chislers, a San Fernando Valley–based club, a few years before they changed their name to its present one, the Choppers. Back then, the club had more members, but some of them were more into bikes than rods and customs. That was where the split came into the picture, and the rod and custom faction started the new club named the Choppers.

The members of the Choppers have a passion for the 1940s- and early 1950s-style rods and customs that inspired many other young car builders of today. The eight members of the club are all artists and craftsmen who got fed up with the "billet" (machined aluminum pieces) and high-tech, high-dollar cars, so they got interested in the history instead. Through old magazines and books, they learned about the past and how the young hot rodders and customizers of the '50s built their cars. Many of the members also have hot rod family backgrounds, and used to go to the swap meets to find parts with their fathers. Thus, they had most of it in their blood already, before they got together.

One of the guys who helped a lot to shape the club is Keith Weesner, who also happens to be an artist who is doing a lot of cool 1950s-style designs for catalogs, T-shirts, and so forth. Keith

When the Choppers plan to attend an event, most of the members will turn up with their cars and bring the club sign. Here is Deron Wright's '41 Ford Coupe in the foreground, right behind the club sign.

Verne Hammond drives his '40 Ford Coupe with its '46 Chevy grille as a daily driver, and the Chevy small-block under the hood makes that easier. Here, Verne is talking to one of the other members of the club, Aaron Kahan.

drives a chopped '50 shoebox Ford, but also has a '29 highboy roadster and a chopped A-pickup in his garage. He is also connected to the custom car magazines through his dad, Jerry Weesner, who is the editor of *Custom Rodder* magazine. Keith grew up reading some of his dad's old hot rod magazine collection, which goes back to the early 1950s.

One of the customs in the Choppers that people always pay extra attention to is Deron Wright's '41 Club Coupe, which was built in the old style. With a radical 6-inch chop and '40 Ford bubble skirts, it received some long and smooth lines that were covered in a flat metallic gold. It has been redone with an Olds '47 grille and repainted in a flat metallic grass green.

Another smooth custom is Verne Hammond's '40 Ford Coupe with a Chevy grille, which sometimes confuses people because they might

think it is a late '40s Chevy instead. Verne painted his chopped coupe in a dark flat green color, as a modern primer, which gives the car additional late-1940s style. The only early-style custom in the club that has been painted with gloss paint is Jon Fisher's chopped three-window '36 Ford Coupe, in a very dark blue color that looks black. Jon built his coupe in an early traditional Harry Westergard style, with a modified front end that has a LaSalle grille and dropped '39 Buick headlights in the fenders. With the '40 bubble skirts and lowered suspension, it rides low with class.

Most of the members of the Choppers are doing their own work on the cars, but on a couple of the customs some of the bodywork (like chopping the tops) has been done by Scott Guildner's Custom Shop in Van Nuys, California. Two of the later-model customs in the club are Kutty

This radically chopped '50 Ford belongs to Keith Weesner, who is one of the more active members of the Choppers. The '50 Ford has also been modified with frenched headlights and painted in a flat wine-red metallic, which gives the custom an old-fashioned look.

Verne Hammond is the owner and builder of this '40 Ford Coupe with a '46 Chevy grille. The chopped coupe has a classic custom roofline and was painted in a flat dark green metallic. Frenched headlights and a set of Caddy "Sombrero" hubcaps complete the look.

Pictured are three Choppers Coupes lined up with Verne Hammond's '40 Ford in the foreground, Jon Fisher's '36 Ford in the middle, and Deron Wright's '40 Ford in the background. Note the LaSalle grille on Fisher's car.

Noteboom's '52 Mercury in red and silver, and Mike Ibbetson's '58 Pontiac in blue metallic. Kutty Noteboom has a real custom background, because his dad is Jim "Bones" Noteboom, who used to work for Larry Watson in the early days. "Bones" is still building stunning customs and has been a winner at the big shows for years.

Young customizers around the world are following what people like Wright, Fisher, Hammond and the others in the Choppers Club are up to with their cars. Old-style customs are coming back, thanks to today's new generation of customizers.

The Choppers is one of the clubs that gives young rod and custom builders lots of inspiration, and not just in the United States. Inspired by United States car magazines, customizers in Europe, Australia, and Asia follow the trends that are created in Southern California. They also travel to Southern California to check things out for themselves at events like the Rat Fink Reunion, held at Mooneyes in Santa Fe Springs, California; West Coast Customs in Paso Robles; or the Oakland Roadster Show. New clubs have been formed in many countries, so the early-style custom club scene is growing daily. Every year at the Paso Robles event you can see at least a few new clubs from the West Coast area, and there is a long list of established clubs represented as well.

Another L.A.-area club that is nearly the opposite of the Choppers is the Sultans, of Long Beach, which has been around since the early days. The club was formed in the late 1950s in Long Beach. During the late 1960s and 1970s it was more or less on idle. It was Dave Ellis who got the club moving again in the 1980s, and he is still president of the club, which now includes more than 80 members. The club and its members are very active, so you can see their cars at most of the West Coast events. The rules state that cars have to be of a

Jon Fisher's '36 Ford Coupe is a good example of an old-style custom built today. The chopped coupe has many modifications, including louvered hood sides, LaSalle grille, fender skirts, and whitewall tires on steel wheels with "flipper" hubcaps. Jon has a small-block Chevy under the hood.

1969-or-earlier model, and most members have late-model, full-size semi-customs dating from 1955 and 1965. Fords from the late 1950s and GM cars from the early 1960s are very popular among the members. Lately, some have even started building customs out of station wagons, including '61–'62 Chevys and '55–'57 Chevy/ Pontiac Nomads. The use of air-ride suspension has made a big difference among semi-custom builders, and that includes many of the Sultans' members. With air-ride, the car can be dropped nearly on the frame for show, but still be "pumped up" to a normal ride height.

The Sultans arrange a couple of their own events every year, the biggest being the street show in Bellflower during the first weekend of June. They conduct it in cooperation with the city of Bellflower, and a street is closed off for the show. With sometimes more than 500 cars, it is a very big event.

The club is also involved in the Signal Hill Show in Long Beach, which donates some of its proceeds to organizations helping battered women. The members congregate often, but their big get-together is a barbecue in October. To keep everybody in the club informed about what has been going on, a club magazine called *Cruising News* is published.

George Evans is one of the spokespersons for the Sultans, and he is well known for his black '64 Ford Galaxie semi-custom. Lately he has also built a two-tone '64 Pontiac Grand Prix, with air-ride suspension and a dark brown metallic paint. There are a few chopped '50 Mercs in the club, and one of them is Larry De-Wise's candy red ride with Buick side trim. Bud Rogers used to drive a very nice deep red, chopped '50 Mercury also, but today he drives a just-finished '47 Chevy custom in candy orange. When it comes to the body-work on many of the club members' cars, the same name keeps popping up, and that name is

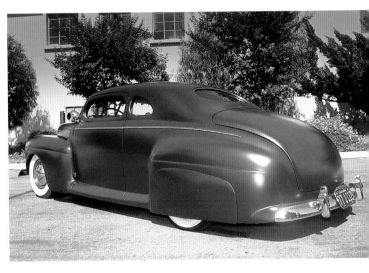

The rear look of a chopped '41 Ford coupe like Wright's is something very classic. The lowered Ford has a set of '41 Ford bubble skirts to cover the rear wheels, which makes the long lines even longer. Rounded corners on doors and trunk were tricks that the early customizers introduced.

George Evans' latest project is this '64 Pontiac Grand Prix, which was given a mild customizing. Dave Ellis is the guy who handles most modifications of the Sultans' members' cars. This Pontiac was modified with air-ride suspension, to get that nice low look.

Mike Doyle. He is a member himself, and he takes care of a lot of the modifications on his friends' cars at his shop in Long Beach.

New clubs are turning up everywhere today, but it is mostly the younger-generation enthusiasts in their early 20s who are forming the clubs. This is a positive trend, because without them customizing would die out. Some of the older generation custom guys have a hard time accepting the new-generation rockabilly kids, with their half-finished rides in primer. But there is one thing they keep forgetting: history is more or less repeating itself. Most of them have a trunkload of tales about how wild they were during the early days, when they first got into building cars. The new, younger club members are experiencing the same things today, and they will help the customizing trends and traditions continue on.

Another old member of the Sultans who keeps on building new customs every year is Bud Rogers. His latest project is this late '40s Chevy. The top was chopped and body cleaned plus the headlights frenched before it was painted in orange pearl with red striping. Whitewall tires and chromed "bullet" caps make the picture complete.

Duane Barbie named his '57 Plymouth after the famous Chuck Berry tune *Nadine*. The pink Plymouth has been given a mild modification with a tube grille and some pinstriping. The hubcaps are the stock '57 Plymouth, which many customs used in the early days.

During the Bellflower event you can see rows of '40s and '50s Chevys parked along the closed-off street. The Sultans work together with the local police department to arrange this yearly event.

Ola Thorslunds' '55 Mercury

Ola Thorslund is a second-generation rod and custom builder, who grew up with the right kind of magazines in his hands. His father has been the president of the Swedish Street Rod Association for many years. Thorslund took the long way when he started with his '55 Mercury custom. To begin with, he bought a very rough car that was in need of a lot of rust repair, but it had a history. It was a custom in the '70s, so it was a good buy for him. During the seven years it took him to finish his Mercury, Thorslund also got involved with creating the Swedish version of Kustom Kemps of America. Their club magazine is called "Lead News" and by sending a copy to Gene Winfield, they got in contact. In 1994, when Winfield visited Sweden and Stockholm for a show, he continued contact with Thorslund and came to his garage to check out the progress of his custom. It took Ola a few more years to finish his first custom, which was chopped 3 inches, with the rear glass was dropped down under the rear panel. The rear fenders were extended around 10 inches and modified for a set of '56 Chrysler taillights; in addition, a set of long '49-'51 Mercury "bubble-skirts" was modified to fit. The front end came from a '55 Ford with a bigger grille opening, filled with a '55 DeSoto grille on a homemade grille bar. To add a lower look to the front, the wheelwell lips were dropped down a bit. When Ola bought the car it was missing the motor and transmission, so he purchased a 400 Ford Cleveland motor, plus a C6 transmission in good

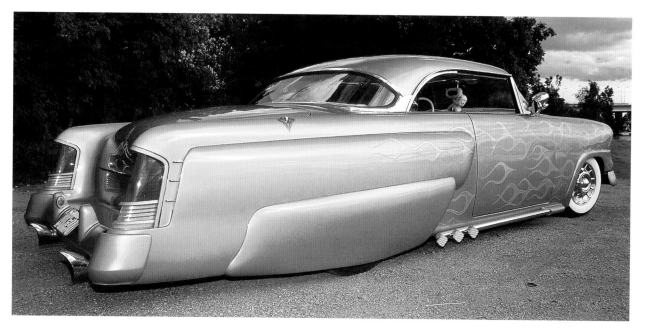

It took Ola Thorslund about seven years to finish his '55 Mercury, because when he bought the car it was in need of rust repair and he had to replace most of the floor. After that, he was able to get into the customizing, starting by chopping the top 3 inches. The front end is from a '55 Ford that was modified with a wider grille opening and a '55 DeSoto grille with a new, homemade grille-bar. The front wheelwell lip was extended for a lower look and the steel wheels have Caddy hubcaps. With the air-shocks all the way down in the rear, the '55 Mercury becomes very low and long. The rear fenders were extended about 10 inches and Ola also modified them to fit a pair of '56 Chrysler taillights. The bubble-skirts are extended and modified '49–'51 Mercury skirts that make the car look even longer than it actually is. Both the front and the rear bumpers are from a '56 Chevy. Bengans Billack in Åkersberga sprayed the lime green metallic, and Ola got some help from his dad to create the flame layout.

shape. With everything detailed, he dropped the motor in the chassis and began preparing the body for paint. The lime green metallic was sprayed by Bengans Billack in Åkersberga, but Thorslund and his dad, Olle, did the flame design themselves.

To make it easier to drive the custom, Ola also installed a set of air shocks, so he could raise the car for normal driving. Bilskräddarna in Solna upholstered the interior over a '70 Caddy front seat and a Chrysler Valiant rear seat. The young Thorslund's first project came out so well that he has been winning trophies at most of the shows he has attended in the last few years. Custom car building is growing all over the world and Scandinavia is one of the stronger areas for young, new builders.

ABOVE: The interior was stitched by Bilskräddarna in Solna, with white and green tuck and roll over a '70 Caddy front seat. A high Lokar shifter was installed to shift the Ford C6 automatic transmission.The dash is mostly stock but it does have some add-ons, like switches for the air-shocks and an air-pressure gauge.

The original engine/transmission combination was missing when Ola bought the car, so he had to find something that would fit both his wallet and the vehicle. A Ford 400 Cleveland engine in good shape with a C6 automatic transmission was just perfect for it. With the exception of an MSD ignition, the engine is near stock, but detailed with a Caddy-style air cleaner on top.

Index